Irene Melo

What Would You Do?

2014

What Would You Do?
Irene Melo

Visit www.irenemelo.com or www.amazon.com to order additional copies.

ISBN: 0615959032
ISBN 13: 9780615959030

This book is dedicated to
Jennifer Moemeka & Elizabeth Figueroa
Two amazing women in my life...

*True friendship is hard to find,
and I'm blessed to have your wisdom to help me grow.
You define the true meaning of friendship.
Thank you for always being there for me.*

*God knew what he was doing when he placed
you in my life.
I'm one lucky lady!*

Acknowledgements

A special thanks to:

Editor of Content
David Adamson

Editor of Patois Dialogue
Delroy Thomas
Tonya Dorman

Editor of Grammar
Lisette Crespo

Photographer of Author Photo
Christina George

Printing Company
CreateSpace an Amazon Company

What Would You Do?

Prologue

Recap of the Novel

"How Far Would You Go?"

Jazzman Garcia, a vibrant and talented Latina, has been working her way to achieving her dreams behind the scenes in the music industry at Irie Land Records in Miami, FL. She has been able to appreciate success in the entertainment industry, where success can be hit or miss.

A year ago, Jazzman's mother passed away from cancer, causing Jazzman to throw herself into work, avoiding the reality that her mother was gone. Jazzman's father had abandoned the family when she was a little girl. So now, although hardly a child, she feels like an orphan and out of place in this world.

Jazzman tried to find solace and meaning in her life through her spirituality, but she constantly asked, *Why? Why my life?* Her best friend, Kim's doorstep was often where she would find herself when her thoughts grew out of control. It was Kim who planned a trip for them to go to Puerto Rico hoping that the time with Jazzman's grandmother would ease the feelings of loss and rejuvenate her friend's heart with joy. Let's take a look at what changed for Jazzman during that trip:

For Jazzman, it's why they call Puerto Rico 'la isla del encanto'/'the island of enchantment'. Nowhere in the world can you find a better climate and the best tasting food as far as she is concerned.

After the delicious dinner, Kim and Jazzman are full from traditional home-style cooking. The ladies go for a walk around the block to enjoy the island breeze and burn some calories. Their walk through town is educational for Kim. Yet for Jazzman, it's insightful as she relives moments she shared with her mother in her hometown.

During the walk, it hits Jazzman that some kids spend their whole childhood without knowing a mother's unconditional love. Growing up she witnessed several kids either raised without a mother or with a mother not involved in their lives. Being in her mother's birthplace gives her a new perspective and she begins to develop a deep appreciation for the times she shared with her mother.

Her discovery leads her to the realization that life is going to be very different from this point on. Gratitude is her new way of life for the time she had with her mother. God has never given her more than she can handle, but this time she asks herself, "how much more can I take?" She responds, assuring herself, "He knows my limits. So I will keep walking by Faith, since that is one thing I know I can do."

The trip helped put her life into perspective, but there were other things brewing back home, such as her relationship with her close friend, Tyson. Tyson and Jazzman met as study partners at the University of Miami. At that time, Jazzman was in a relationship, so Tyson worked his way into her life as a friend, secretly hoping for more. Jazzman now considers Tyson one of her closest friends.

When Tyson opened up to Jazzman about his true feelings for her, it made Jazzman skeptical of his motives, because at the time

Afrique a well-known reggae artist had just proposed to her. This made it hard for her to trust Tyson's admission of stronger feelings. Besides, how could she take Tyson seriously when she knew he was a 'playa'? She brushed it off as his male competitive edge reacting to another male in her life.

Even without Tyson's admission of feelings, Jazzman had her own doubts because her connection with Afrique started as a one-night stand. From the moment their eyes locked there was an instant attraction. They soon discovered that they shared a deeper connection, both lost their mothers to cancer. A loss they carry in their hearts. After that night, Afrique tried calling Jazzman, but she never got the message. They each thought the other didn't want anything more. They both believed in 'everything happens for a reason', and knew that chance encounter was a moment they would carry as an imprint on their hearts. But a month later, when Jazzman's job sent her to Jamaica for Sumfest, Afrique surprised her backstage.

Hours before they reunited, Afrique had his house set up for a candle light dinner. When he found himself at Sumfest, he had no idea if his master plan to win Jazzman's heart would work. He questioned how someone he just met could have his emotions all messed up. The dinner was a sign to Jazzman that he put thought into wanting to be with her. Or was she settling due to moments of loneliness invading her life for too long? She knows that sometimes her thoughts lead her to the wrong guy, but she's hopeful that Afrique is different. Let's relive the night they reunited:

> Afrique pulls his hands away from her eyes, and Jazzman can't believe it. She never expected this type of surprise. The kitchen is fully decorated with roses. The lights are dim, and the candles at the center of the table are burning. Shirley Biscuits are on the dinner plates and the champagne glasses are filled with milk.

She thinks to herself. *He put thought and effort into this, and he had no idea if he would run into me tonight.*

Her eyes are watery. "You did all of this for me?"

He smiles, knowing he is probably out of the dog-house, "I don't see any other female here."

"What are you trying to do, make me fall in love with you?" Jazzman is about to sit down when he grabs the chair, and pulls it out for her to sit.

He brings his arms around her waist and whispers in her ear, "That wouldn't be a bad thing now would it?" Afrique takes his seat and looks at her.

She acknowledges the look and says, "I'm glad you found me tonight."

He gazes deeply into her eyes, "I've been waiting patiently for you to come to Jamaica."

Holding back the joyful tears she softly responds, "On that note, I say let's toast." She holds her glass up and he does the same. She says, "Let's toast to... let's toast to us."

The glasses chime and they take a sip of milk followed by a bite of the biscuit.

Afrique gets up and walks over to her, he pulls her chair away from the table and kneels down to her.

She asks, "What are you doing, Afrique?"

"Relax." He begins to kiss her neck, kissing every weak spot as she moans in excitement.

She whispers, "I missed you."

He teases her, "I don't think you did."

She begs, "Please, I want to feel you inside me."

He asks, "You sure you can handle me this time?"

She gets up to where her pelvic area is leveled with his mouth and she says, "I don't know, let's find out."

After sharing a very romantic night, the two wanted to spend more time together. Fortunately for Jazzman, the record label extended her time in Jamaica, to seal an important deal. They wanted her to sign a hot up-and-coming reggae artist named Oriba.

During her week in Jamaica, Afrique and Jazzman spent their time getting to know one another. By the end of her stay, they were both questioning their love. How can one feel so much passion and love for someone they just met? When their week came to an end, as luck would have it, Jazzman missed her return flight to Miami. She decided to surprise Afrique and took a taxi back to his home. But she was the one who got the surprise of her life when she saw Afrique embracing another woman, who then entered his home with a young boy. The boy must have been his son, and the woman was the boy's mother for sure. Why did he hug her? And why did they all go in the house together? Hurt and confused, Jazzman returned to her hotel without confronting Afrique.

You see, during Jazzman's week stay in Jamaica Afrique accidently disclosed that he had a child. Jazzman was okay with him being a dad, but the way in which the information was revealed led her to question his integrity.

So upset, Jazzman checked back into the hotel and called her best friend, Tyson. Once again, Tyson came to her rescue. He calmed her down that day and he surprised her the next morning by showing up at the hotel with a killer red gown in hand for her. Tyson had planned her revenge, by escorting her to a reception being held in honor of Afrique. This time, Afrique received the surprise of his life when he saw the woman he called his own, Jazzman, on Tyson's arm...and at his event! Let's go back to that night at the reception:

> Afrique controls his anger by taking a deep breath and his stiff lips manage to motion, "Jazzman, what are you doing here? I thought you went back to Miami."

She is pissed, but she says with pride, "Looks like you thought wrong. After all, it didn't take you long to forget about me."

Afrique is confused, "What are you talking about?"

Jazzman is really upset and tries hard to hold back her tears. "Tell me, why were you so nervous when I walked through that door?"

It is killing him not knowing what she is trying to insinuate, so he tries to play it off, "I was startled to see you, that's all. You said you were going back to Miami and now here you are, here, with him."

Jazzman looks over at Tyson and says, "Of course he would put this on me. He still can't tell me about his wife. I'm sorry...I mean...His family that he betrayed to be with me. Uuuhhhhhhhh...You know what Tyson, I think we need to leave. Maybe we should take our friendship to the next level." They turn to walk away.

Afrique reaches out for her, "Jazzman, where is all of this coming from? What's going on? Talk to me."

She turns and says, "There is nothing more to talk about. I have to go." She points to the stage. "I think you need to go as well, it looks like your ceremony is about to begin."

When Afrique tries to reach out for her again, Tyson steps in this time and gestures for him to back off.

From the moment Afrique met Tyson, he had questioned the friendship with Jazzman and how they really felt for one another. Afrique's insecurity comes from his own similar experience with his son's mother, Jackie. His son, Desmond, was conceived one night years before when Afrique and Jackie impulsively decided to sleep together, taking their friendship to the next level. Jackie becoming pregnant changed everything. Their friendship was tarnished for sure. They stayed connected for the sake of their son. Afrique was afraid to share this history with Jazzman just yet. He did not want to mess things up when he was just getting to know her. And yet his actions pushed her into the arms of another man without understanding how it was happening. What happened that night between Jazzman and Tyson?

When Jazzman and Tyson get back to the hotel, he walks her to her room and says, "I'll see you in the morning."

She asks, "Where are you going?"

He begins to wonder why she is inquiring when he answers, "To my room."

"You shouldn't have done that...you could have stayed with me."

"I didn't want to impose." He kisses her on the forehead and says, "Get some sleep and I'm right across the hall if you need anything."

As he begins to walk away she calls out, "Is it okay if I stay in your room for a while?"

She can't see his face but he has a grin that reaches from ear to ear, he wipes it away with his hand before he turns to answer, "I'd love that."

When they enter the room, Tyson takes off his jacket and shoes. Jazzman gets comfortable too as she takes off her shoes and jewelry. Tyson grabs the remote and turns on the TV. He sits on the bed and wonders, *what next*, as he flips through the channels.

Jazzman thinks to herself, *I've got to give him credit. He went out of his way to cheer me up. I think deep down inside we want each other, but we both don't know if it will work. Well, if it didn't I think we would still have our friendship. What am I talking about? If it doesn't work our friendship would never be the same. I don't know what I would do without Tyson as my friend.*

Jazzman asks lying on her stomach, "Can you give me a massage, please?"

"Okay, just don't try anything." Tyson grabs some lotion and begins to massage her back.

As his hands work on the knots she whispers, "That feels so good."

Her words turn him on and he helps himself as he begins to kiss her neck, and she allows him to do so as she moans in agreement. He brushes his fingers through her hair making her weak. She is a prisoner to his touch as she is pressed against the bed. He's on top of her in control of her body. She calls his name in a whisper and he responds by slowly working his way to her mouth. He gently turns her around and she slowly strokes her fingertips up and down his chest. The repetition of her hand makes her arm ache and she realizes it is a little sore from when Afrique grabbed her arm. The moment brings her thoughts back to Afrique, reality sinks as she says, "We can't do this."

The next morning when Jazzman went back to her hotel room she was startled by Afrique's voice when he says, "Where were you last night?" He had somehow gotten into her hotel suite and wasted no time wanting for Jazzman to answer. After back and forth arguing it was clear that nothing was going to get resolved.

When Jazzman returned to Miami her focus was her career, because she nearly jeopardized it by having a relationship with Afrique. Upon her arrival, her boss informed her of her new assignment as director for Bimma's music video on his upcoming release, "In Her Shoes". She refocused her whole being on her job and hard work was nothing new to Jazzman. She loved her work and she would often get lost in it and lose track of time. But her thoughts always caught up to her at night when she would rest her head on her pillow and come to the realization that she felt lonely without a man.

On the upside, through all of Jazzman's trials and tribulations she always counted on one person, Kim. Kim was her wild girlfriend, the kind of woman that every female loves to have in her life to live vicariously through her. Even though Kim was the one always at the clubs, she also had a low self-esteem due to her rough childhood. Her mother had countless men in and out of her life, but when her mom finally gave herself to the Lord, it was a little too late for Kim. Kim was set in her rebellious ways, which had become the norm. It would take years of life's lessons and years of therapy to get her to see that something inside her was missing. Something inside her was making her substitute what she needed with materialistic things as well as her promiscuous ways. Yet, there seemed to be hope for Kim because her combination of kindness and street smarts has helped her to be a big sister to Jazzman. She always told Jazzman the truth even when the truth hurt, because that's what real friends do for one another. Kim had a splendid way of putting Jazzman in her place and vice versa. It's what forced these two friends to tell one another time and time again, "You were right."

Jazzman often went to Kim for advice. Kim thought she had Afrique figured out. But there was one time when both women were wrong about Afrique. They thought he was married, but it would be Tyson who set the record straight through a strange encounter.

One night Kim, Jazzman, Tyson, and Jordan (Tyson's best friend) were at a nightclub celebrating Jazzman's upcoming video directing job.

When they were done partying, Tyson took the women home in his car and Jordan went home on his motorcycle. That night, Jordan ended up in a motorcycle accident and was in the hospital for a few weeks.

One morning, while Jordan was still in the hospital, Tyson went to Jordan's apartment to feed his dog. There was a knock at the door and there stood a woman. Tyson heard so much about her from Jordan and he had his doubts. She lived with her son's father, supposedly just living together for the sake of their son. She would visit Jordan for long weekends but Jordan was starting to get wary of their relationship and wanted her all to himself. When Jordan turned to Tyson for advice, he would respond, "Leave her." Yet that moment when she stood there, he put that aside to explain what happened to her man.

Tyson took her to the hospital. The whole ride there he could not help but feel like he'd seen her before and while at the hospital he figures it out:

It finally hit him why she looks so familiar. He asks, "What is your son's father's name?"

She is confused as to why he is getting personal, "Afrique—"

Tyson interrupted her, "The singer...right?"

Startled, she says, "Right but how do you know that?" She thinks for a minute. "I saw you at the club a few weeks ago in Jamaica with a woman, right?"

"Yah, that was me."

Jackie takes a deep breath, "Small world."

"Who you telling? I don't know what to say, I'm speechless."

"What I want to know is what role you play in all this?" Jackie asks still surprised.

"Jazzman is a good friend of mine. You said...you mentioned you have good news. Is it over?"

Jackie senses the importance he is placing on her answer. She remembers Jazzman being really upset with Afrique, and the hurt showed in her eyes. She gave that look to Jordan when he wanted to give up on their relationship.

Jackie answers, "Yes. Please let her know..." She pauses for a second. "...Tell her not to let him go. He is a good man. He deserves to be happy, as happy as I feel when I'm with Jordan."

Tyson cared about Jazzman too much to keep this to himself. He told her about this crazy twist of fate. As soon as she heard, Jazzman wanted to rush to the phone and call the man she was in love with but she decided to wait and pray he reach out to her and make that move. She used the time to allow the wounds to heal. Afrique finally called her. He was prepared for her to fight him on his request to meet, so he was shocked when she accepted.

Once they each had a chance to talk about what really happened things began to look up for their relationship. They reunited knowing they wanted to be with one another. They understood what the other had been through and they understood each other's lifestyle. Their relationship was on a path that led to a marriage proposal.

So, before you begin your journey with "What Would You Do?" here is an excerpt from the last chapter of "How Far Would You Go?" which takes place at Jazzman's and Afrique's engagement party.

$\backsim\!\!\!\!o$

Jazzman looks elegant in her backless dress with her hair styled and her make-up flawless. She feels like she is back in high school attending prom, and the thought sends a tingling sensation through her body.

The limousine pulls into a familiar boating pier, and she has a funny feeling about where she is heading.

When the boat reaches her favorite island so many feelings begin to hit her. She's nervous, anxious, excited, surprised and amazed at how Afrique found her favorite place.

She thinks to herself, *How does he know? I can't wait to ask him if someone told him about this place or did he find it on his own. If he found it that would be so crazy.*

Thoughts of her daddy rush to her mind as she reminisces about the times she spent on the island with him. Her favorite part is the bridge that overlooks the long narrow waterfall. It is an amazing site, at one time she feared it, but it was there she first heard the story of a young girl named Cinderella. Her dad told her the story as if it took place on this island. Needless to say, the story helped her overcome her fears. Each time she went there, she would throw a penny in the water and wish for her Prince Charming. The thought brought goose bumps to her exposed skin.

Her thoughts are interrupted when she hears music. She turns to the man who is directing her to where she needs to go and she asks, "Is that an orchestra playing?"

He smiles. "Yes it is."

"Why are they playing here?"

"They are here for you."

Paralyzed for a second, Jazzman takes a deep breath to help her relax. She whispers, "Me?"

She takes a minute to listen to the music and the sound is somewhat familiar to Jazzman, but she is unable to place her finger on the name of the song. Until she hears his voice singing to the melody of the music, it reaches her soul and she is overwhelmed with joy. He is singing 'The Woman, Her Soul'. A song he wrote and shared with her the night they first met.

She reaches a point where red and white roses are beautifully designed on the ground, which lead to everyone who is waiting her arrival. As Jazzman approaches, the crowd notices her and she recognizes so many familiar faces.

She thinks for a few seconds, *Oh no, I hope Afrique is not surprising me with a wedding. He should know better than to steal that moment from me. If it is, I don't know what I'm going to say or do.*

Everyone begins to cheer "Surprise!" She smiles in response, but is still unsure what this all means, thinking, *what is the surprise?*

Afrique yells into the microphone, "There she is, my beautiful wife-to-be."

She thinks to herself, *please Lord, don't let this be my wedding.*

Afrique hands the microphone to a man who takes over in singing with the band.

He walks over to Jazzman as he welcomes her with a kiss and everyone claps at their embrace.

She whispers in his ear, "What is this? What's going on?"

He looks into her eyes and answers, "It's the official announcement of our engagement. Surprise my love."

Jazzman melts with happiness, "OH…That's so sweet. I have to be the luckiest woman alive. Thank you baby." She hugs him one more time to say, "I love you so much."

As Afrique and Jazzman walk through the crowd, they greet family and friends. Everyone takes turns congratulating both on their engagement.

I feel like I'm in a fairy tale, she thinks to herself. She finally has a good look at her fiancé, and she is overwhelmed at how handsome he looks in his gray Armani suit.

She tells him, "I can't believe you pulled this off. How did you do it?"

He answers, "I can't take all the credit. Tyson helped me with all the arrangements."

"Wow, I can't believe it." Jazzman says blushing.

"I've been told the only way to pull something like this is to not tell Kim."

She starts laughing, "You got that right we can't keep secrets from one another."

One of the waiters interrupts them to have a word with Afrique. He excuses himself and walks with the guy.

Kim walks up to Jazzman, "So, I'm told I can't keep secrets."

Jazzman gives her a hug, "That's okay they're just jealous because they don't have a friendship like ours. So, you must have heard that Tyson and Afrique pulled this off all on their own."

Kim smiles, "I sure did."

"I can't believe they did this."

"And you thought he didn't love you anymore."

"I know can you believe it. I was going to talk to him today about the way I was feeling. I'm glad he spoke first and told me he had a surprise for me."

Kim gives Jazzman a hug. "I'm glad it worked out. I'm so happy for you; you deserve all the happiness in the world."

Tyson joins them, "So, what's going on over here? Are you two talking about how you want to get with me for a threesome?"

Simultaneously the girls push him and say, "Whatever, you couldn't handle one of us let alone both of us."

They all laugh and then Tyson says, "Hey Kim, do you mind if I pull Jazzman away for a minute?"

Kim answers, "No problem. I'll talk to you two later."

Kim walks away, Tyson starts to walk in the other direction, and Jazzman follows asking, "What's up?"

Tyson motions, "Let's walk and talk."

"Tyson, I don't think that's a good idea. I just got here."

"It's cool. I already talked to Afrique about pulling you away."

"Oh, okay. Say no more, I sense another surprise. Let's go." Jazzman is still trying to digest all the excitement she is feeling.

Tyson asks, "So...were you surprised?"

"I sure was. I still am. I honestly can't believe the two of you pulled this off. Thank you for all your support."

"You don't have to thank me girl. You know that's how we do."

Jazzman senses Tyson's nervousness, "Is everything okay?"

As they approach the bridge, Tyson turns to her and says, "No. I'm worried about you."

Jazzman asks, "Why?"

He explains, "I want to make sure you are doing the right thing."

"Of course I'm doing the right thing. I wouldn't have agreed to marry the man if I didn't love him."

Tyson gets the courage to say, "Listen, I'm gonna tell you like it is and how I see it. I've known you for a long time and no one makes me smile the way you do. They say people should start as friends for a lasting relationship. We have that and more. At least I think we have more. I want more for us than just friendship. I don't know if I'm making any sense. I do know that you have only known this guy for, what, not even a year and the two of you are getting married. This is crazy, Jazz. Have you thought about what you are getting ready to do? Do you realize that you are going to fight for this man's love while thousands of women are throwing themselves at him. We know what this industry does to people, Jazz."

Tyson thinks about what he just said, "Jazzman, I'm so sorry. I didn't mean to do this at least not here, not today, but it's been on my mind."

Jazzman feels torn, upset and unable to think.

"Say something, Jazz."

"Tyson, we've never acted on our feelings, we've played around, but that's different. I feel like now that someone has shown interest in me, you want me. You yourself mentioned being somewhat jealous. Are you sure you've thought about what you want from me? Actually, what is it that you want from me?"

"Honestly, I want us to be together because I don't think..." He takes a minute to think about what he is about to say.

Jazzman is heated, "What Tyson? Say what you have to say."

"I don't think anyone can love you the way I do. There, I said it."

Jazzman grows numb and confused on how to feel. "Why are you doing this to me? Why now?"

Tyson quietly says, "Because I love you. All jokes aside...there's no other explanation than...I love you. You know, planning all this for you, I kept thinking this should be me. I kept saying, 'I should be the one with Jazz'. So, here I am. I could not live with myself if I didn't speak up."

Jazzman tries her best to tell him how she feels, "Tyson, I love you too, but why now. You've had so long to step up your game and make a move on me. I will admit to you, there were times I've felt the same way, but your ways have prevented me from taking you seriously. I'm still having a hard time taking you seriously because you are telling me this now, when I'm engaged and about to get married."

"I know...wait...You mean...you've felt the same way too and you never said anything to me. Why haven't you?"

"Come on, how could I? All your concentration has been on living a single life? You've been with so many women, and I can't compete with that lifestyle."

Tyson tells her, "Newsflash...You would have won, hands down."

Jazzman asks, "So where do we go from here?"

"I don't know...why don't you give it some time and think about it? What do you say? Can you at least do that?" He reaches over to hug her.

She hugs him back, "Yes, but I think I have a better idea. Maybe I should pray on it and let God help me find my way. After all, I'm not getting married today, RIGHT?" She asks pulling away.

He smiles in agreement and says, "Right."

She adds, "Good because the last thing I need are two men planning my wedding without me having any say in the arrangements? By the way, you know I would have been upset if this was my wedding day, right?"

He smiles to himself because what she says, confirms there is still hope for him, "I hear you. Let's get back to the party, because I'm starving."

Midway toward the crowd Tyson turns to Jazzman and reaches into his pocket. She grows nervous for a second, but when she notices a blindfold, she is a little disappointed. Tyson blushes knowing what she is thinking, "I've been requested to put this on you before we reach the party."

She smiles and says, "Okay, but don't let me fall."

"You know I've got your back."

His statement brings Jazzman to get lost in her thoughts.

Laughing, Tyson says, "Get your mind out the gutter."

"I did not say a word."

"You didn't have to. You know if there is anyone who can read you, it's me."

Tyson helps her all the way to center stage of the party, and Afrique takes it from there. Everyone is facing Jazzman and Afrique when he takes off her blindfold. They all yell, "Surprise" as some of the crowd moves left and the other half moves right for what awaits her is an ice sculpture of her mother and Afrique's mother.

The tears surface at the corner of her eyes and before she could wipe them away Afrique kneels down on one knee and asks, "I have dreamed so many nights of marrying the perfect woman and here you are. You opened my heart to love, the love shared between people in love."

He pulls out her engagement ring. He had asked her for it the other day. He told her he needed to take it to the jewelers for inspection and cleaning.

He continues, "It is with honor and in the presence of everyone here that I ask YOU...Jazzman will you be my wife?"

She is in shock when a bigger diamond is placed on her finger. There are several sniffles from family members and friends, as everyone waits for Jazzman's response. Jazzman feels the pressure for this is the real deal. She knows that once she commits, it will be for life.

She finally asks herself the question she is afraid to raise. It's a question she asks anytime she meets a quality man, *Can he make me laugh the way Tyson makes me laugh?*

She thinks about it for a few seconds and then feels a headache forming. She looks over at Tyson. He could sense her hesitation, but he also knows how she reacts under pressure, at least he knows there is still hope for them.

Jazzman responds to Afrique, "There is no question in my mind that you are the love of my life and the one that made all my wildest dreams come true."

Everyone coughs at her last remark thinking it's a little too much information. Jazzman realizes what she just said and how people might interpret the remark. "Come on, people."

Everyone laughs.

"What I mean to say, what I'm trying to say is I'd be honored to be your wife."

Her answer crushes Tyson's aching heart. He did the only thing left for him to do, *Lord, help her find her way to my heart, because she represents the spirit of my soul.*

Jazzman and Afrique embrace as everyone cheers for their happiness. Tyson joins in but he is stunned by her acceptance speech wishing he were the one holding her. They all form a circle and watch as Afrique and Jazzman dance to "The Woman, Her Soul".

Chapter 1

"What Would You Do?"
1997

MIAMI, FL
Jazzman and Afrique

"Thank you. This has been one of the most amazing days of my life." Jazzman hugs Afrique and he embraces her with a tight squeeze.

"I hope this is the beginning of many more to come." He looks into her eyes and they smile instantly, thinking the same thing, his last 'word' and how they wish they were home right now getting lost in each other's love.

When the boat reaches the other side of the lake, Jazzman and Afrique say goodbye to the last few guests from their engagement party and their driver opens the door to the Rolls-Royce. As they both settle into the car and it is just the two of them, her headache becomes persistent. So she closes her eyes resting her head on Afrique's lap.

She is overwhelmed by her situation with Tyson and her fiancé, wondering how her life will play out. She hopes that her relationship with Tyson can remain stable without all the drama. Although with Tyson, what you see is what you get and she has to admit she is the same way. She also feels the tug of war between Afrique and Tyson knowing that Afrique can handle only so much of Tyson. She wonders if one day Afrique will attempt to sever their relationship, which scares her to death. She hopes that the two men will grow on one another, each secure with their own position in her life.

However, a memory creeps into her mind, back to the night she went out with Tyson, Kim and Bimma after her first video shoot. It was that dance with Tyson that had her vulnerable to his touch:

> Tyson and Jazzman move their way to the dance floor as the song 'Y Hubo Alguien' by Marc Anthony begins to play. The song represents their relationship as they pretend that only feelings of friendship exists between them, but the way they danced tells a different story.
>
> As their bodies connect, their gaze states 'I want you'. From the outside looking in one would say they are more than friends, as their body movements communicate 'you are mine'. On the dance floor their true emotions are exposed. It intensifies as he draws her close and their bodies nearly become one.
>
> For Jazzman and Tyson, music is their addiction, and it serves as their secret way of expressing their true feelings, as she lands with her backside against his mid-section. Their moves travel to a place of making love, yet a place their mind tells them to continue life as just friends.
>
> As they dance, there is an undercurrent of passion between them. When he holds her, their bodies tease one another as they move to the beat. Her hips scream for more and he obeys by gracefully placing his hands around her to spin her around. It's a beautiful site the way he controls her body, drawing her close during certain lyrics, causing her body to hit a climax of pure bliss.

Once again, she asks herself, *Can Afrique make me laugh the way Tyson makes me laugh?* She closes her eyes even tighter and a tear escapes as she answers her own question, *No he can't.*

She remembers something else that happened that night. What Tyson said to her when she was broken-hearted about Afrique. She tries to convince herself, *Well, Tyson has hurt me, too. No one is perfect. I guess Afrique hasn't made me laugh that way yet. I'll have to give him some time that's all. He makes me laugh, just not the same way. I'm sure that when we have as much history as Tyson and I do, we will share that same connection.*

But her thoughts do not let her forget what he said after he hurt her feelings, and what happened when they left the club:

> Tyson opens the car door for her and whispers in her ear, "I'm sorry."
>
> His words send shivers down her spine and she is unable to stay mad at him, "I forgive you."
>
> Tyson reaches in for a hug to call truce, but it catches Jazzman off guard. Their lips accidentally touch, causing another awkward moment between friends. Meanwhile, Kim is watching, smiling.
>
> She waits until they both get into the car and says, "Can the two of you just get a room, please! If money is a problem, I'll pay for it."
>
> Tyson reaches over to the back seat to hold down Kim's legs and begins to tickle her on her stomach as he says, "Why don't the three of us get a room."
>
> Jazzman shakes her head, "Kids, can we please go? I need to get my ass to bed; I feel a headache coming on."

A headache like the one she has right now...formed by not confronting her own truth? Or are her emotions playing a trick on her?

As Jazzman's head is resting on Afrique's lap he drifts into his own thoughts thinking, *Something seems strange. I can't put my finger on why Jazzman seems so far away. I wonder if she is mad that I made this a surprise engagement; women do get funny with this stuff. I hope she still wants to marry me. Then again I still wonder about Tyson and her. I'm not sure that's a friendship I want to encourage. I have my doubts and do not want to live with that for the rest of my life. Maybe I should start plotting to shut that relationship down. I hope she is still happy. Then again, forever is a long time and I do not know if I'm cut out for forever. Maybe I'm just getting cold feet. I need to stop. We aren't getting married tomorrow. There is still time to sort through these questions. One day at a time. I'll talk to her about these feelings before we tie the knot. I want to clear the air before we take it to the next level.*

At the same time, Jazzman takes a moment to pray, *I know one has to be careful what they ask for, but Jesus if he is not the one for me...please help me see it before we step into marriage. Give me a sign or signs and help guide me to what I need to see and feel. And as always, guide me to my purpose in life. Thank you, Lord.*

MIAMI, FL
Tyson

"What now?" The party has ended and Tyson feels helpless and lonely. He stops at a bar near his house, to forget about his thoughts.

"What will it be?" The bartender asks wiping down the counter.

Tyson answers, "A shot of Hennessey and a Heineken."

He watches as the bartender tends to his drinks. Tyson drops a fifty on the counter and tells him to keep the drinks coming.

Tyson takes his shot and guzzles down half of his beer as the events of the day play back in his mind. *I can't believe she picked*

4

him. I can't believe that I let her walk away. I wish I told her sooner how I felt. Forever is a long time for those two to be together and I don't think they are capable of lasting that long. He is not good enough for her. I wish she could see that we belong together. We are right for one another. I feel it. So many women have come into my life, but no one compares to Jazz. She has everything I want in a woman. The mind, the body, her sex appeal, the way we click and when I take in the scent of her perfume…it just leaves me suffocating. We complement each other. What more could I possibly need.

Tyson drinks what's left of the Heineken and the bartender hits him up with another shot and another beer as he continues to lose himself in his thoughts: *I would feel complete with her by my side. I think she would be the type to keep her figure right, even after three kids. But even if she didn't I would love her anyway. I always knew from the moment I set my eyes on her that she was the one for me. It's that feeling that dad used to tell me about the moment a man sets eyes on the woman of his dreams. Well, I'm not going to rest until I conquer my treasure.*

Tyson guzzles down some more of his beer, *so, where did I go wrong? Maybe I told her too much about me. Maybe that is why she hasn't been able to make that leap of faith and land right in my arms. I want that girl so bad I can taste her. I fucked this one up big time. How did I get here at this bar drinking my misery away and Jazzless? Damn, that sounds corny but who cares. It's my damn thoughts and I will speak the way I damn please. I need to get over this shit. Might as well do it tonight and figure out what's next. Lord, if there is one miracle that I have in my possession it would be for Jazzman and Afrique to part ways. I know that's terrible, but I think what I'm requesting is the right thing for her. I'm sorry Jazz, but I believe in my heart I am what's best for you.*

MIAMI, FL
Kim and Rick

When Kim arrives at her apartment, the place feels empty. She wishes she had someone with her to wipe away the feeling of loneliness, but she is not sure that is the right answer either. Rick is so far away and she wonders what will become of them. She picks up the phone and dials his number.

Rick picks up on the second ring, "Hello."

Kim is all giggles and responds, "Hello. How are you?"

Rick smiles and answers, "I'm good, baby. What did you do today?"

"I went to Jazzman's engagement party. It was amazing!"

Rick responds confused, "I don't remember you telling me about an engagement party."

Kim smiles, "I know, but remember when I told you they had me reserve today but would not tell me why? The big secret was the engagement party. I'm so happy for Jazz. She was beaming with joy, it was just a nice night and it was the perfect way for Afrique to show her just how much he cares for her."

"Wow, that's good…what about Tyson, how was his mood?"

Kim answers, "Surprisingly he was in a good mood. He held it together, but he did pull Jazzman away for a while. I'm dying to know what they talked about—"

Rick questions, "Wait what did Afrique say when that happened? He wasn't upset? He was okay with Tyson pulling her away?"

Kim answers, "—that's what I thought, but it was planned for him to pull her away. Even Jazzman questioned it for a second, but Tyson assured her it was okay. When they returned, the surprise was ice sculptures of Afrique's mom and Jazzman's mom."

"Oh wow, that must have been a priceless moment. I have to give it to him, the guy knows how to lay it on her, but then again he is Afrique…he can pull it off. That's nice. I'm sorry I wasn't your date. I would have been the luckiest man there to have you by my side." His voice was soft, "Did you miss me tonight?"

Kim is surprised by his question, "I did. I would have loved to show you off and introduce you as my handsome date."

Rick responds, "And I would have said correction, this handsome guy is her man."

Kim is startled and unsure if he's playing or being serious. What he stated is news to her, and it excites her. Yet, she somehow doubts it asking, "Are you serious?" Kim could not believe that slipped out. That's what she wanted to say internally to question her state of mind. "I mean really, do you mean that?"

Rick smiles answering, "I'm serious...I meant what I said. I know the distance between us may put a damper on our relationship, but I think during the getting-to-know phase it works. I know for some people questioning this type of distance, the response would be 'hell no'. However, I feel when you really like someone you take the risk no matter what obstacles are standing in the way. We have chemistry and I think it's worth giving it a shot."

Kim has torn emotions on his view. She's not used to a long distance relationship and not sure she can stay faithful. She is a very sexual person. This thing she has with Rick would be unfamiliar territory for her, but if he is willing so is she. It also makes her feel special that he is the one committing. "I say let's go for it. After all there is no one right way of getting to know someone. Some people live with one another for a long time, still don't know each other and are miserable. We do have chemistry. I can't deny it and to not give it a chance would be sad. So, YOU are MY man. When some chick up north wants to get with you, you make sure you let her know that you are MY '*Papi Chulo*' and that you have a chocolate *mamacita* who adores you. By the way I love the way you make her feel, like a lady."

Rick responds smiling, "I like that!"

Kim says, "Oh really? Well, I'd like to add...a lady that needs you because you are good for her soul." Kim can't believe the words she is speaking. Even Jazzman pops into her head giving her that look and the two of them laughing knowing that Kim is not the one to say these type of things.

Rick responds, "Damn, you're good for my ego. When are you coming up here so we can seal the deal?"

Kim answers with a question, "No time like the present. What about next weekend?"

Rick answers, "I say lock the date and I will see you in the Big Apple."

Kim's excitement is heard through the tone of her voice, "Will do! I can't wait to see you and wrap my arms around you. Good night my love."

"Buenas noches mi princesa."

After they hang up, Kim says to herself, "Mmm...I like that...I know what I'm dreaming about tonight."

MIAMI, FL
Jackie and Jordan

Jackie asks, "Are you tired?"

"Not really. Are you?" Jordan asks gently massaging her shoulders.

Jackie, Jordan and Desmond retired early from the party and had just finished tucking Desmond into bed. The three had a long emotional night. It was not said, but it was felt. They turn off the light in Desmond's room and walk into the living room. Jordan grabs the remote and powers on the TV. Jackie snuggles up beside him and he lowers the volume, waiting for her to open up.

"I am tired. It's been a long night, know what I mean?" Jackie looks up at Jordan.

"I do, honey. I know exactly what you mean. Do you want to talk about it?" He asks hoping she will let him know what's on her mind. He wants her to release it, so they can put it past them.

"There are a couple of things I'm feeling. The good thing is that it has finally sunk in. The charade Afrique and I played for so many years is finally over. I finally feel free from those emotions. The hard part is dealing with the emptiness I felt for so many years. We were a family. Not the ideal family, we weren't affectionate to one another, but we made it work for Desmond. Afrique kept saying Desmond wants us together, but that was his fear talking. Afrique's yearning for his father's love dictated how he fathered his son. So we made it work for the sake of Desmond. That's what parents do. But now I realize that is not the best way. A child senses the tension and they feed off that. I'm glad that lie is over, because I have you. I have love! I have a family here with Desmond and you. My heart aches for Desmond because I know he still wants his mom and dad together and I know that will never happen. But I also know that if I show him how happy I am now, he will feed off that positive energy." Jackie is not sure if she said too much. Still, she lets out a sigh of relief for releasing and exposing her feelings.

Jordan hugs Jackie and assures her, "As long as you are okay with it, I think he will learn to be okay with it. Like you said, a part of him will probably always in the back of his mind want his parents together. However, if he sees you happy as well as providing a stable home for him, I have to believe that he will be okay. I'm not saying it's going to be easy, but we will work through it together. As long as we keep the lines of communication open and as long as we are honest with one another, we're good."

"I love you." Jackie wraps her arms around her man and gives him a kiss.

"I love you, too. Let's go to bed." Jordan turns off the TV and he feels more at ease knowing the family that is beginning to form between the three of them is still intact. If it were up to him he would have proposed to Jackie yesterday but he does not want Desmond to feel like he is taking his mommy away from him. Especially when his little mind is still sorting through his daddy being with another woman.

᪗

MIAMI, FL
Kim and Rick

Kim's loneliness gets the best of her as she begins to touch herself thinking of Rick, wishing she were in New York with him right now. As she touches her body in the dark she wonders what Rick would do to her at this moment. Before long she is pressing redial on her phone.

Ricks voice sounds groggy. "Hello."

Kim asks seductively, "Hey you, what are you doing?"

"I was dozing off. Is everything okay?"

"Nope, I can't stop thinking of you. I'm sitting here touching myself wondering how it would feel if you were here. What would you do?"

Kim pauses for a second, allowing his mind to explore and then she continues, "Would you let me fall asleep next to you or would you touch me? Would you lick me like a lollipop or would you kiss me goodnight? Would you cuddle with me, OR lick me like chocolate ice cream taking long strokes with your tongue, taking a sweet bite and letting it melt in your mouth." She asks again, "What would you do?"

"Damn, you know how to wake up a brother. Before I answer, I have a question. Do you want some foreplay?"

"I'm sooo in need right now. I'd say very little foreplay."

"I got you...I prefer chocolate ice cream with hot fudge over a lollipop any day. On the other hand, chocolate ice cream has nothing on you. First, I'll kiss those sexy lips of yours and I'll let you feel how hard I am...you feel that? Tell me, do you feel it?"

She moans, "Yes, I feel you."

"You feel me rubbing against your body?"

Still moaning she answers, "You feel so good."

"Take it. It is yours, but I don't think you're ready, so I'll take my tongue and massage your body. Is that what you like? I'll stop and make you beg for me to return to your needy body. Move your fingers away from your clit. That is my territory and my tongue is ready to explore. If you want to go on the journey you have to beg. Let me hear you beg."

"I'm begging *papi*...mmm...give it to me...can I cum...I want to cum. Let me feel you. I want to scream your name...give me some... please! I'm going crazy...please...please!" Kim lets out a moan because the pit of her stomach is twisting up in knots wanting to explode.

"Here...I'll give you a free sample. I'm sliding in gently...damn you feel so good." Rick smiles as he hears her moan, "Yah, that's what I thought. It's too much for you right? Let me pull it out, for now." As Rick strokes his manhood he continues, "—There is another part of you that is feeling neglected. I'll bring my hands to caress your breasts and let your nipples come to life with my tongue...fuck that, I'm hungry...I want each breast to take a dive into my mouth...as I taste them... you are wrapping your legs around me...you want more of me...I feel it...I want you too...DAMN...you want me to go back South...you feel lonely down there? Are you HOT? You want to get WET?"

Kim expresses, "That sounds so good." I have a confession to make, "I'm already wet, 'cause you've already been exploring inside me and you feel so freakin' good. Do you mind if I take it out for a minute so I may explore some unfamiliar territory and mark it by massaging it into my mouth?"

Rick's body jolts with intense energy, "Damn Kim, be my guest."

Her smile is felt through the phone as she asks, "You feel that? It's my tongue playing with the tip as you look down at me hoping that I keep it warm by stroking all of it in my mouth. No words are necessary. Your eyes are telling me what you want. Mmm...of course, I want to please you, so I gaze into your eyes, in slow motion I give you what you want. Inch by inch...I secure it into a warm place." Kim moans in excitement. She is pleasing herself and her man at the same time.

"I'm going crazy. I want you!"

What started off as a sensual sensation between her legs has escalated with Rick's words causing a spark to ignite within her hungry body. His voice alone sparks her self-pleasure. She wants to explode with satisfaction, but this was no two-minute fix. It's a feeling that has been dormant for years and releasing it will play out best in slow motion enjoying the climax.

"I guess the feelings are mutual. I need you…I need you here with me right now." Kim can sense that he is stroking his manhood and it gives her the power to say, "Cum…cum into my mouth."

Hearing those words allows Rick to explode as she reacts to the chemical reaction. The moment allows their bodies to feel pleasure.

They both let out a sigh of relief. "Damn, if it feels this good over the phone. I know it's going to be off the chain when we actually make love."

Kim smiles, "I know. I can't wait to see you. I miss you!"

Rick says with sincerity, "I can't wait for you to fall asleep in my arms. *Te quiero, mi corazon.*"

"Goodnight and sweet dreams." Kim does not want to hang up but she knows if she stays on any longer she will go crazy without the real thing.

"*Buenas noches.* Sweet dreams, my love." Rick hangs up hoping he has found his match. Although, it scares him to think that her insecurities may get the best of her and cause her to split. It's a fear he has often felt with women, in part due to his mom leaving him at a young age. He has the ability to be patient and take it slow with a woman, sometimes too slow. At times, he has to remind himself once he feels secure in the relationship to be careful not to smother a woman with his love.

MIAMI, FL
Kim

Kim hangs up still wanting Rick. Her thoughts of him take over again. She envisions him touching her again as an explosion rushes through her. She uncontrollably cries out for him. She imagines him responding by pushing deep inside her. As the passion between them heats up, her tears surface once more from the soothing feeling that possesses every part of her naked body feeling unexplainable pleasure.

She visualizes him flipping her body around and continues to make love to her. He demands, "Say you want me!"

She obeys, "I want you! I want you Rick!"

He brings her body into a butterfly position for deeper impact. As the sensation penetrates through their bodies, the temperature between them rises. The feeling reaches their souls confirming together they will make sweet paradise.

The thoughts become so intense that Kim has to stop herself. She's been here before thinking of a guy wondering what he will feel like and then the real thing never matches up to her thoughts. She hopes that the way he makes her feel in her mind will have the same impact when their bodies actually unite for the first time.

NEW YORK, NY
Rick

At the same time, Rick finds himself not able to fall back to sleep. He shakes his head, wondering how he is going to manage the rest of the night without his Kim. His head is ready to explode. "What a long night it will be," he says wishing he could snap his fingers and make Kim appear in his bed. For now he has to dream and falling back to sleep is a nightmare.

In the morning when he wakes up, Kim is still on his mind, so he allows his thoughts to think of what he will do when he makes love to her for the first time. He envisions his body blending with hers in the motion of love. He continues the movement while admiring her body. Her curves allow small trickles of sweat to flow down her back.

While his body is in motion, he wishes a camcorder were rolling to capture a moment that is worth watching again and again. The way he presses his body against hers causes her to look back at him. The vision of such a beautiful view excites him and her sexy lips entice him. The passion in her eyes assures him that he is satisfying her. They keep the momentum flowing until they reach their climax of powerful orgasmic bliss. The moment of satisfaction causes them to collapse and hold each other tight, soaking in their intimate obsession for one another.

Chapter 2

MIAMI, FL
Jazzman

Ever since the engagement party, the thought of getting married is becoming all too real and scary at the same time for Jazzman. It's times like this she wishes for her dad's presence, to talk to her about men. Then again, she realizes how ridiculous that is since he was certainly no male role model. Her emotions have been all over the place all month, as if she is constantly on her period. And when her thoughts get like this, Jazzman often thinks of going to therapy. Only today she is actually following through. All she needs is someone to talk to. She needs someone to help her sort out her feelings and settle emotions that have been persistent since her mother's passing. She is also hoping this will help her deal with her anger towards her father for abandoning her at a young age.

Jazzman has been nervous all week about going to therapy, not really sure what to expect. She almost called to cancel several times, feeling uneasy at the thought of running into anyone she knows at the therapist's office.

When she enters the office she is relieved to find no one waiting in the visitor's lounge. She didn't want anyone making assumptions of her mental health. She finds the soft music welcoming, somehow soothing. The therapist exits her office to introduce herself as Helen

Wright, a middle-aged Caucasian brunette with glasses. She requests that Jazzman fill out the necessary paperwork while she photocopies her insurance card.

Jazzman found the process intimidating, having to answer so many questions. It made it all too real. She is moments away from releasing things she has been through in her life, the things she has bottled up for a long time and it's scary. When she finishes the paperwork they both walk into Helen's office.

Helen asks with a soft-spoken voice, "Jazzman, welcome and what brings you here today?"

Jazzman is trying to figure out how to respond and finally answers, "Well, several things...it's been over a year since my mom passed away and—"

As Jazzman pauses, Helen says, "Oh...I'm so sorry."

Jazzman continues, "—thank you. It's been hard dealing with it."

"I'm sure. Well, you can begin wherever you'd like." Helen says looking at Jazzman so she can begin.

Jazzman takes a deep breath, "So, I guess I will start with my dad. Well...actually...I have to give you some history. I grew up in Miami and my mom raised me. My dad left when I was a little girl."

Helen calmly asks, "How old were you when he left?"

Jazzman answers, "—about seven years old."

Helen responds, "I see, continue."

"The reason why he left...well...my mother kicked him out because he was abusive...but...when he was gone, that was it...we never discussed him again. I was afraid to bring up his name knowing the pain he caused my mom." Jazzman's voice begins to crack but she holds back her tears. She gets emotional thinking of the pain and emptiness she is feeling.

Helen signals to where she can grab some tissue.

Jazzman reaches for one and continues, "Well, since she passed away, my dad has been on my mind and I have all these mixed emotions. I feel alone in this world without my mom, because I am an only child. She kept me grounded. Now she is gone and I feel stuck somehow. I'm feeling my dad's absence and wondering why he never looked for me or tried to contact me again. You see, after my mother's funeral it took me months before I could go back to the cemetery. When I did, I discovered flowers were placed on her stone and it was from my dad. After years of nothing, just flowers and a card left at her grave? I don't get it!"

Helen asks, "How did that make you feel, Jazzman?"

Jazzman pauses for a few seconds to hold back the tears, but she is unable. "I was sooo angry...confused...mad and I've asked myself over and over how could he leave the flowers and not look for me. I needed him. I still need him. What's weird is that even though I'm mad...I'm also happy."

Helen interrupts, "Why are you happy?"

"Happy because finally a sign of him...happy to know he is still alive...happy to know I might connect with him or see him and finally get some answers. It would have been nice to have him comfort me at the funeral, but he wasn't there. I can't believe he left those flowers and hasn't looked for me. How does a man live with himself knowing he has a daughter and left her fatherless? Who does that?"

Jazzman thinks for a second, "A COWARD...that's who does that... no, not a coward just someone who doesn't care about anyone else, just himself...I'm MAD...I'm SO MAD in here." Jazzman clutches her hand to her heart. "I don't know what to do with this pain and this anger. I don't want to have to hold onto this hatred especially when it is due to someone else's selfish behavior. I want to heal. I want you to help me heal. I want to get over this madness and move on with my life." Jazzman lets out a sigh, "I've never felt I could tell all this to any-one...I feel like I need closure...Maybe I need to let him go and move on with my life. He's around, but it's obvious I'm not on his list. At the same time I miss that unconditional love and I need him. I need a dad."

Helen questions, "Jazzman, have you ever tried looking for your dad?"

Jazzman feels embarrassed as she wipes away the tears, "No, I haven't. Well, when my mom was alive, I felt like I could not betray her that way. Yet, every time I watched a talk show that reunited families, I would say to myself I wish that were me. I would have this dream that I was called on that show. They would tell me they found my dad and that he is a changed man. But then I would say to myself, if he were a changed man he would have looked for me. I used to write down the toll free numbers that displayed after the shows and tell myself 'I will call'. Then I would think of my mom and what he did to her. I would ask myself, do I really want to reunite with a man who not only hurt her, but also abandoned me? Obviously, my answer was 'no' all the time. Now, here I am."

Helen asks her a hard question, "Do you want to look for him now?"

Jazzman is unsure of how to answer and she sits there for a minute wondering until she responds, "I'm afraid of what I might find out. Sometimes the truth hurts and I am too weak to handle the truth right now. So, right now...I don't think so. I'm still angry."

Helen questions, "When he left the flowers, was that the first you've known of him since he left you at age seven?"

Jazzman answers sadly, "Yes, that was the first time and the part that sucks...it wasn't for me. Do you think him leaving the flowers is a way to get my attention, to let me know he is still around?"

Helen asks, "I don't know. What do you think?"

Jazzman replies, "I thought about that before and honestly, not wanting to get my hopes up, I pushed that theory aside. I also think maybe he found out too late about her passing. So, when he did find out, he left the flowers. I guess I'm trying to give him every possible excuse, but then I just get so mad at how much he hurt me. Then I wonder, does he even have a clue as to how much he's hurt me over the years by not being present?"

Helen tries to pull out more information from Jazzman. "What do you feel he has done to you?"

Jazzman's eye's well up with tears, "For starters, I remember watching him hurt my mom, when she didn't do anything wrong. She did not deserve it. He abandoned me when I needed a father in my life. His behavior caused me to question how a man is supposed to treat a woman."

Helen asks, "After your dad left did your mom have any other relationships? Were there any abusive partners?"

Jazzman thinks, "Well, she tried to keep that part of her life private. She would send me to Kim's house. I know of one relationship she was in, and he was controlling. However, he helped with the bills, so she dealt with it for a while. I think sometimes that's why I am clueless about relationships. I used to sit and observe couples just trying to figure it out. Even though I would tell myself I would not be with an abusive man…I was worried that somehow I would end up with one. What also bothered me about my father…he wasn't there for my graduations, poetry recitals, high school plays, softball games and birthdays. Every year…every birthday that passed was another year he wasn't present. THAT HURT! Each Christmas and birthday was painful…and every year that passed…I still had hope and every year…nothing. I used to hear that song on the radio by Randy Vanwarmer, "You Left Me Just When I Needed You Most" and it reminded me of my dad."

Helen smiles, "I remember that song. So, what else, Jazzman?"

"I guess I'm looking for closure. I feel like he's the only one who can answer my questions. So I guess I need to dig deep and find out if I really want to search for him now…now that my mom has passed. I don't have to worry about hurting her or worry about how she will feel if I look for him. I'm scared. I guess I'm scared no matter what I decide to do. Then there is uncovering his side of the story. Maybe he won't care about me or care about getting to know me. Maybe he never cared. Maybe what I find out will hurt me worse than what I'm feeling now."

Helen suggests, "How about one step at a time on deciding whether or not you want to search for your dad. If you decide not to, you don't need him to have closure. You can do that on your own and I can help you reach that goal. But, let's say you decided you want to search for him. Take me through the steps you would go through in preparation, from searching to the final encounter."

Jazzman thinks long about that possibility and how she would handle searching for her dad. "My first step would be finding a reputable organization to search for him. My second step would be to meet with them and ask questions about reuniting families. I would want to know various outcomes of connecting families with situations similar to mine. I would like to know both positive and negative experiences. Third step would be if they find my dad I would want them to provide me with an update on his life, if possible. Then find out if he wants to reunite. The fourth step would be to prepare for the actual meeting with my dad and make sure I have all my questions lined up for him. The fifth step would be once we reunite to ask him the hard questions about his absence in my life." Jazzman stops to think if there are any steps she is missing and concludes, "That would be my way of working on closing this chapter in my life and moving towards a new beginning."

Helen asks, "What about dealing with your feelings? What about counseling? What about a relationship with your dad after you two reunite?"

Jazzman could not believe she left that out, "Of course...yes, all of that. All this anger I have...whatever I find out afterwards... we would definitely need it. Well, if he would agree to it. And if we reunite I would want a relationship. But with that said, he would have to want the same thing. Maybe I won't want a relationship with him, depending on what I find out. His answers to why he left and why he never looked for me might be my clue to stay far away from him."

Helen questions, "What if the agency informs you that he does not want to see you?"

Jazzman feels her heart drop and is extremely uncomfortable with Helen's question. "That would hurt. It would be like he is abandoning me all over again." A lump forms in Jazzman's throat and she needs a minute to regroup.

Helen eases her emotions by responding, "Remember, if you don't want to find him or if he does not want to be found, there is another way to resolve your dad's absence. Like I said earlier, you can still move on and have a healthy life without him present. I believe you can get to that peaceful place in your life with some coaching. How does that sound?"

Jazzman smiles with a mixture of relief at sharing her thoughts for the first time and hopeful that she'll find some answers to her long standing questions about her father. "Sounds like a plan. There is something else that is bothering me. Well, since my dad hasn't been present...and now that I have a fiancé...I'm doubting the relationship. I'm trying to make sense of my life. With so much that has happened this last year...I'm really not dealing with it. So, I need some guidance on how to cope with my decisions. I'm here to talk through and attempt to fix whatever doesn't feel right. I want to figure out what I'm feeling and why. Am I making any sense?"

Helen gently smiles giving her a reassuring look, "You have come to the right place. Therapy means different things to different people and people need therapy for different lengths of time. We can evaluate your progress from week to week. I want to provide you with the tools you need to maintain a healthy life. So, for today I think we will stop here."

They wrap up on last minute housekeeping items on her session and Jazzman walks out of therapy feeling relieved. She is happy with her decision to give therapy a chance in her life.

MIAMI, FL
Jazzman and Kim

[Music Blasting]

Jazzman and Kim are driving to the gym with the top down, jammin' to a new reggae joint on the radio called "Tour".

Kim turns down the music asking, "So, how was therapy? Did you get anything out of it or did it feel like it was a waste of time?"

"Well, I walked out of there with more questions than answers, but it felt good just to let everything out. Somehow during the visit I ended up feeling comfortable sharing so much. She didn't do much talking, but maybe she can help me begin to glue the broken parts of my life back together. Although, I'm not quite sure how that's going to happen. I can't believe I opened up in that way."

Kim is in shock, "Really?"

Jazzman quickly glances at Kim wanting to see her facial expression. Therapy hadn't worked for Kim when she tried it for her troubled past. She softly responds, "Really. It was good, Kim. It almost felt like I was giving someone else my problems. I was releasing things that I had been hanging onto for so long. Before, I felt lost with all the stuff in my head. I still do, but it feels good to know I am doing something about it. I hope this therapist will help me get to the bottom of the sadness that I feel in my heart. I feel stuck and I feel like all my hopes and dreams can't fully surface until I heal from my broken past—" Jazzman was quiet for a moment and then says, "Wow, I just had a moment."

Kim is curious, "You got all that from one visit? I've never been able to find a therapist to help me like that. How did you strike gold at your first visit?"

Jazzman responds, "I researched therapists in the area and I asked people if they knew of a good one. That is how I ended up at her office. She came highly recommended. However, I too, was willing to talk, I needed to talk...Lord knows I need it. I guess it helped knowing I was speaking my thoughts out loud to someone who I knew would not judge me. I don't know what the end result will be, but I'm glad I took the first step to finding out. I think it might help you, too. Kim, I hope you allow yourself to try again. You can't shut down at those sessions; you have to allow yourself to open up and begin healing. I know you carry resentment from your childhood, but don't allow those moments in time to define your whole existence. I know I've done that but I'm trying to get beyond that. Allow the past to heal and it will make you a stronger woman. At least, I have to keep an open mind about this process. Am I making sense?"

Kim's stiff body loosens up as her eyes become glossy, "I know. You're probably right. I've been thinking about it lately…how I used to fight the therapist and not allow myself to get the right help; or I would shred the therapist to pieces before giving her or him a chance. So, you are going back, right?"

"Yes, I am. I have another appointment set up. I want to make good use of my sessions so I'm starting to think about stuff I can bring up at my next appointment. I'm scared, excited and hopeful all at once. You know what I found interesting? She told me to start writing to my mom in my journal. So, at first I thought…weird, but now I'm getting excited about doing that. She wants me to write as if I were talking to her. I can't wait to start. I'm just working up the strength to make that happen because I'm worried about how I will feel afterwards."

Kim responds, "That's interesting. I like her idea. I think you'll be fine."

Jazzman adds, "The best part about therapy is that I have someone listening to me who doesn't have a clue who I am and like I said earlier I don't have to worry about her judging me. I hope she works out. Sometimes things appear cool the first time around, but you never know with these things. The vibe felt right. I hope she will help me get deeper into what triggers me and discover things about me. I want to enjoy having her as a therapist to bounce my life story off of and to feel at peace with my life experiences."

What Jazzman does not realize is just how much that last statement resonates with Kim. Kim has a thing about people judging her lifestyle. All the years she's gone to therapy she has heard and read that a therapist does not judge your character, that they help you discover the demons within. But hearing Jazzman say it was like an affirmation allowing her to move forward to get the help she needs.

Kim's inquiring self asks, "How are things between Tyson and you?"

Jazzman grows uneasy, "Honestly, I'm still working through some things he said and still trying to understand it all. So I can't answer that right now. But you already know you will be the first to know."

23

Kim and Jazzman arrive at the gym and she parks the car in a shaded area. They grab their gym bags and head in, walking straight to the locker room.

Kim asks, "Do you think you can give me your therapist's name and number? Would you feel funny if I saw the same person?"

"I don't mind at all."

"Maybe I should give her a shot and finally deal with my past head on."

Jazzman's excitement takes control, "Really? You will?" Jazzman gives her a tight squeeze. "I'm so glad. I know you've been fighting it for so long, but if you truly commit this time I think you will find your own answers. I'm glad we've had each other's back all these years."

The two change into their workout clothes and walk into the studio for an Abs Class. Before opening the door to the class they notice a sign:

Coming Soon!!!
POLE DANCING 'WORKOUT' CLASS
Get **SEXY** and **FEEL** yourself into shape
Sign Up @ the Front Desk!

The two of them look at each other and both begin to laugh, reading each other's thoughts.

Jazzman says, "This sounds fun! What do you think?"

Kim replies, "I say lets sign-up! I'm ready for some pole action."

They laugh again and take a detour to the front desk before joining their class.

MIAMI, FL
Jazzman and Kim

After the gym, Jazzman decides to go shopping for her getaway trip with Afrique and Kim joins her to shop for her own trip to see

Rick in New York. They park the car in the vicinity of South Beach to hit the boutiques on Ocean Drive.

As Kim shuts the passenger door she says, "Jazzman I have a confession to make."

As Jazzman locks the car, her facial expression is full of curiosity, "What happened? Is everything okay?"

Kim smiles nervously, "What do you know about Buddhism, the practice of Buddhism and meditation?"

Jazzman responds slowly, "I don't know much and I don't have an opinion about it. Why? Do you want to take a class?"

Kim smiles. Jazzman knows her too well. "There is a woman who comes to the salon who practices Buddhism and I've been asking her questions about it. I'm interested in learning more. I think it's another outlet to help me with my past. It might help me come to terms with it. Basic religion has never registered with me and I think this might. I feel a connection to it. I feel like it could help me. The way I look at it, it won't hurt to try it. What do you think?"

Jazzman thinks for a minute answering, "Hmm, I wasn't expecting this from you. I'm sort of speechless. I don't know what to say. Tell me more about it. Then I can give you my honest opinion."

Kim responds, "Fair enough. Well, here is what I know so far: it's merging the mind with the body. It's about finding God through meditation, and treating others the way I want to be treated. I see it as a way of really getting to know who I am and to challenge my thoughts. I think that Buddhism will help bring peace to my past. It's about healing. At least that's sort of how the woman explained it to me."

Jazzman responds as they walk into the shoe store, "Hmm...so, does this mean becoming a Christian is out of the question?"

The two women stop their conversation when they spot a sexy pair of red heel sandals also available in orange. Their philosophy, if you find something you like and it's available in various colors, buy one of each. Kim also spots a shoe that has a blue, brown and white pattern.

Kim looks at Jazzman with the patterned shoe in hand, "Are you thinking what I'm thinking?"

Jazzman smiles, "With a pair of jean shorts, it'll look like we have 'legs for days'."

Kim adds in patois, "We can swing from da pole and tease um til' dem beg for da pumpum."

Jazzman sings, "Touch me tonight. Make me shiva...work da middle til mi heat like fire..." She dances and adds, "I can't forget my jam...Flex...Sex...look how long you have dis rude girl a sweat."

Kim laughs, "Lawd have mercy, we wicked."

The two giggle to the thought of driving men crazy and getting free drinks, when the attendant comes up to them and asks, "Can I help you ladies?"

Jazzman answers, "A pair of 7's in all of these."

Kim adds, "A pair of 8's in all of these too."

The attendant smiles, looks at all the shoes and says, "I'll be right back."

While waiting, Kim comments, "To answer your earlier question, I'm not sure I'm cut out to be a Christian."

Jazzman is a little disappointed, "Ouch...I was looking forward to us going to church on Sundays. I guess that ain't gonna happen."

Kim gives her a sad puppy look, "I'm sorry, are you mad at me? We can still go to church together sometimes, as long as you don't try to convince me that being a Christian is the best thing for me."

"I would never do that to you. I believe that everyone should believe in some form of God. It's up to the individual and what works for them and their life experience. Just don't try to walk into a Catholic church 'cause they will ban you with your promiscuous—" Jazzman is interrupted by the store attendant.

"Here you go, ladies. Let me know if you'd like to try on anything else." She smiles and walks away.

They respond, "Thank you."

Kim playfully calls out to Jazzman in Patois, "Yuh ass."

They laugh as they try on the first pair of shoes. Jazzman continues, "Like I was saying, as long as you are seeking spiritual guidance, I'm good. I just want to see you happy and make peace with your past."

Kim is relieved. "Thank you, Jazz, for understanding. I was nervous about telling you, but I think I'm going to find comfort in meditation. I think it will help me let go of my negative thoughts and come to terms with what I've been through."

The two get up and look in the mirror and admire the shoes. After trying on several pairs they 'check out' with their favorites and 'check into' vacation mode thinking of the '*muy caliente*' nights ahead with their men.

Chapter 3

MIAMI, FL
Kim

As Kim secures her seat belt and waits for the airplane to take off, her thoughts drift back to her first date with Rick in Puerto Rico. It was when she had first begun to consider that she might have finally met someone who knows how to treat women with respect. She is allowing herself to open up to him. Normally, she would not have given him a second glance, but something about him seems different. She has decided to enjoy the ride getting to know him. She longs for the feelings of love and security in a relationship. As the airplane begins to move down the runway Kim closes her eyes and remembers the end of her first date with Rick:

> They both take their shoes off, feeling the sand between their toes and go for a stroll along the beach. Rick is different from her usual dates, the ones she meets at the club who provide romance, but nothing serious. She feels special with him. She loves the calm feeling she possesses when she is around him. He brings out her confidence.

Rick senses that Kim is not the type to reveal too much of herself. He asks, "So how has your stay been here in Puerto Rico?"

"I love it. I wasn't expecting to meet anyone."

He loves her answer. It let him know where he stands, "Is it safe to say 'thank you'?"

She smiles and places a kiss on his cheek, "Does that answer your question?"

"Wow." Rick, not expecting that, playfully falls down on the sand, and pulls her down with him.

She laughs, "You have got to be the craziest date I have ever had in my life."

He looks into her eyes, "Do you think we could do this again?"

She nervously answers, "I don't know. We do live far apart, but anything is possible."

She gently kisses him on the lips and places another on his neck.

He asks, "Mmm. Do you mind placing one more of those, right here?"

She gives him another kiss on the other side of his neck.

"Mmm. Do you mind if I ask you for another one right here?"

She gives him a few tap kisses on the lips; he playfully works his tongue into her mouth. She plays along allowing his tongue to unite with hers.

Then she slowly pulls away, "I'm sorry." She is unsure of this moment, feeling as if she doesn't deserve his kindness.

He whispers in her ear, "You don't have to apologize."

"What time is it?"

He looks at his watch and smiles, "11:30 and I promised to get you home before midnight. I don't want folks calling the cops on me."

They walk back to the motorcycle in silence and the ride to Jazzman's grandmother's house seems too quick. When they arrive, he turns off his bike. As he helps Kim off, she says, "This would be the part where I invite you in."

He smiles, "But this is the part where I would have to decline because it's not fair to put a cheap price on quality merchandise."

"Oh." That took Kim by surprise, and she feels embarrassed.

"Please don't take what I said the wrong way. I want you to know I really enjoyed myself tonight, and I can see us having amazing times together. Why rush a good thing? I wouldn't mind getting to know you, if you are game."

Kim still can't believe the man standing in front of her as she asks herself, *is he for real, or is this a game?*

With time, she learned that this is not a game and maybe Rick is for real. She has waited so long for someone to treat her right and maybe it's finally happening. The best part, it came at a time when she wasn't looking for love. She had been focused on helping her best friend through a hard time. She definitely has enjoyed every moment she has shared with him. She is not sure what the future will hold with their long distance relationship but she is willing to risk it with him. The feelings she has are definitely heading in the right direction.

BROOKLYN, NY
Kim and Rick

While Rick steps out to the store for a few things, Kim gets comfortable at his place in Brooklyn, NY jamming to the various radio stations. She is enjoying it so much that she grabs her cell phone and dials Jazzman's number to brag about it.

Jazzman answers, "Hello."

"Hey girl, what's up? How are you?" Kim sounds energetic with the music playing in the background.

"I'm good. Where are you? Are you at the club this early in the day?"

Kim laughs, "No, I'm at Rick's place. I called you because I keep forgetting to tell you that I love the radio stations up here. I like WBLS! And Hot 97 is HOT! You weren't lying! They even have your kind of music."

Jazzman gets all excited unaware of a dedicated station. "They have an all reggae station?"

Kim laughs, "NO! That club mess you listen to, you know...you left me...I need you...come back to me, why did you leave me all alone. You know TKA, Corro and Cynthia."

"You know what...I know you listen to it, too, on the down-low so don't even try it. I won't let you forget 'Diamond Girl' in Puerto Rico with your *Rico Suavesito*." Jazzman laughs at Kim in a joking manner.

Kim joins in on the laughter. "Okay, you got me, but on the real I really love the stations up here. I LOVE New York!"

Jazzman is in agreement, "I know it is a beautiful city. I love the vibe up there. They do have a great selection of stations to choose from. Have you listed to Ed Lover and Dr. Dre in the morning? Those guys are hilarious."

"I have...they are too funny. Well I got to go, my *hombresito* is coming back soon and I want to be ready for him when he returns."

"Sounds yummy. Enjoy yourself *y cuidado*."

"What?" Kim asks unsure of what she heard.

Jazzman smiles, "You better start learning some Spanish...it means be careful."

"Oh, I knew that. Here is mine..." She says in patois, "Lata ear."

The girls laugh and hang up.

⌒〇

BROOKLYN, NY AND NEW YORK CITY, NY
Kim and Rick

Since Kim loves to shop, Rick takes her to all the cool spots in the city. First, they hit the fashionable clothing stores on Flatbush Avenue in Brooklyn. Then, they make their way to the city to shop on 5th Avenue where all the designer stores are located. While they are in the vicinity and per Kim's request, Rick brings her to Jazzman's favorite store where her favorite movie took place. He takes a picture of Kim outside the building next to the sign 'Tiffany & Co.'. Their next stop is midtown on 7th Avenue for the DKNY sample sale. Kim had no idea what it was until Rick put her onto it. It's the reason why they did not shop at the uptown DKNY store. Once they are done fighting the crowd at the sample sale, they make their way downtown where all the funky shoe stores are located. While in the area, Rick decides to bring her to Chinatown on Canal Street, so she can see the knock-off designer products. Kim makes a few purchases there.

Rick seems to know her taste and throughout the duration of the shopping spree he helps pick out just the right stuff. Surprisingly, she feels as comfortable shopping with Rick, as if she were with Jazzman.

After a long day, they go out for dinner at Windows of the World in the World Trade Center. One of Rick's boys works there and hooks them up with a table without a reservation. Rick thought it would be cool to have Kim experience the restaurant's rotating floor, which one can't feel move until looking up from time to time. Kim did exactly that and with each glance her eyes are exposed to another view. She is amazed at the scenery and it's a great way for her to take in the skyline of New York City.

Following dinner, Kim and Rick get cozy in a private room at the restaurant. The picture window in front of them gives them the perfect view of Manhattan.

She realizes that Rick really seems to know what makes her tick and each time he does something kind for her she feels more comfortable with him. "This is so incredibly breathtaking. I never knew a place like this existed."

Rick smiles, pleased at how well things are going and happy that he could introduce her to new things. "I'm glad you like it. I'm really enjoying myself with you, Kim. I like the vibe between us and I can't wait to share more moments like this with you."

Kim seems a little uneasy and Rick wonders if he said too much, and wonders if he came on too strong with his feelings. "What's wrong?"

Kim still appears uncomfortable, "Oh no, it's nothing you said. I enjoy our time together, too, but...my head is pounding."

Rick knew this could happen being so high up. "Do you need me to get some aspirin? Or do you want to go back home?"

"Actually, I have some aspirin in my purse. Do you mind getting me some water?"

"Sure, babe, I'll be right back." Rick kisses her on the forehead and looks for some water in the next room.

Kim tries to relax by rubbing her temple and reflecting on her time with Rick so far, hoping it will take the edge off the pain. She thinks back to last night when he cooked her dinner, the way he treated her and the way he made her feel. *'I wonder if this is what Jazzman first felt with Afrique when they first met or am I in competition to feel loved?'* Before she can put any more thought into it she hears him getting closer.

He returns with a glass of water asking, "I hope this helps?"

Kim takes the aspirin with some water. "Let's just relax right here for a minute and hopefully with you holding me, the pain will go away."

"Now, that sounds like a plan, but I hope you are not getting sick of me already."

Kim smiles, allowing her eyes to flirt with his, "Not a chance. You are not getting rid of me that easy."

He loves her smooth way of getting him excited, which is causing conflict with Rick wanting to take it slow with her. Although, he wouldn't mind hittin' it right at this moment, causing an adrenaline rush with the possibility of getting caught. "Mmm...do not start something you can't finish...right here...right now."

"Maybe we need to. After all we have the perfect view of the city, and an amazing sight in here. I think we should merge the two and let the fireworks begin." She gets on top of Rick despite her aching head, as her inner thighs are resting on his lap. He has a wonderful view of her breasts and she has a breathtaking view of the city. Kim is enjoying her moment of feeling on top of the world.

"What are you going to do if someone comes in the room?"

"If they can't enjoy the show, they can walk right back out." She answers as she places gentle kisses on his neck. Kiss by kiss, as her lips touch his skin the room temperature begins to rise to the occasion.

"Mmm. Don't stop."

Knock...Knock!!

Kim jumps off Rick and the two start laughing as Rick yells, "Yes!" No one responds. Rick walks to open the door but no one is there. They laugh some more.

Rick comments, "I think that is our cue to bounce."

NEW YORK CITY, NY
Kim and Rick

Kim asks, "Where are we getting off?"

"59th Street," Rick answers placing his hand on her leg.

They are taking the A train from Brooklyn to Manhattan to see an off-Broadway show, 'The Soul of Harlem', set in the 1970's.

They get off the train to walk a couple of blocks to 59th Street and there is a short line, moving quickly, to get into the theater. Their seats are several rows back from center stage. This is Kim's first off-Broadway show in New York and she wonders if he senses her excitement as she tries to conceal it.

He is enjoying exposing her to new things in New York. She brings excitement into his life and he feels his manhood in full swing around her. His past relationships with New York women never lasted more than several months. He never felt as connected and caring as he feels with Kim. He never dreamed he would meet someone in Puerto Rico, let alone a Miami *mamacita*.

After a few minutes of waiting, Kim could not contain her excitement, "I'm so thrilled I can't wait!" This morning, she had read a glowing review in the New York Times. She read it was based on a true story. So she is eager for the curtain to rise and the tale of Harlem Renaissance to begin.

Rick smiles and lightly presses his lips against hers, "I'm glad you're here with me. I enjoy your company."

Without even thinking about it Kim opens up and responds, "Thank you. I've loved this day and I love being here with you."

As the curtain begins to rise revealing the stage, everyone simmers down to lose themselves in the storyline of Harlem. It opens to a prostitute, a young, bony African American woman (Woman 2), her face etched with the effects of years of selling herself to get high. The moment is frozen as the spotlight shifts to a beautiful, younger voluptuous African-American woman (Woman 1) singing a heart-wrenching, soul-attacking song, 'I Know Your Struggle'. The singer represents the prostitute in her youth before prostitution and drugs became her way of life.

The actress looks right at the crowd and says loudly, "Don't judge me! You don't know why I act the way I do. You don't know what I've been through in this Godforsaken place. Tell me, 'what would you do' if you lived through my trials? Before you answer that, let me give you a piece of my history."

Woman 1
Full of elegance, style and class
I was a woman that men adored
If a man took me out to dinner
An intellectual conversation we would have

I allowed men to open doors
And treat me like a lady

Woman 2
I'm a woman that sells her soul
Because I have nothing else to offer
I ask a dealer to feed my drug-infested body
But, I have no dough to supply
A piece of ass is my peace and offering
In exchange for that toxic sin

Woman 1 and 2
So…where…did…I…go…wrong
Look at what I've become
Lost…in…my…shadow
I…do…not…recognize…my…own…face
Look at what I've become
Helpless… Homeless…Worthless
Look...At...What…I've…Become!

Woman 2
Who shall I blame?
The dad that was never present?
The uncle who gave himself permission to molest me?
Or the boys at school who claimed I was easy?
As I offered my body for a small piece of affection
Their love never lasted that long

Woman 1
I could not control my life as a child
As a young woman, I had choices
I should have listened to the strong women of Harlem
Who said no good would come if I gave my love to a thug
So look at what I've become

(Whisper)
Help me...Help me
Give me strength
Wrap your arms around me
Help me...Repair my soul

Woman 1 and 2

Lost...in...my...shadow
Look at what I've become
I...do...not...recognize...my...own...face
Look at what I've become
Helpless...Homeless...Worthless
Look...At...What...I've...Become!

Woman 1 and 2

Thank you, Lord, for answering my prayers
You guided me through my darkest nights
You restored my faith that night I almost died
On 125th Street overdosing on crack
Laced with a potion I did not recognize

Woman 1 & 2

I've grown to learn my lesson
Every day a battle to stay alive
I was addicted to drugs, sex and alcohol
Now, I feel the power
To change my destiny
Here I stand before you, a woman you recognize
Secure...Wiser...Stronger
I'm now addiction FREE!

Your-Love-Is-My-Overdose...NOW!

The song cuts through Kim's skin, chilling her to the bone. The lyrics brought her back to her childhood. As a young girl watching her mother's apartment become a revolving door for all the men who took a piece of her mother's womanhood. Man after man, she would see a part of her mom get lost in sexual pleasures. She had wished that her mother had been able to focus on her as a child, instead of the men she entertained.

Kim swore she would never be like her, yet to some degree she has become that insecure woman. Kim tried hard to avoid it. However her relationships were always with controlling men, just like the ones her mom brought home, men who made her insecure, tearing down her self-esteem. The type that she allowed to use her for one thing or another, guys that brought drama to the home and did not bring anything to 'the table'. When she learned her lesson, she stopped dealing with broke brothers, only dealing with guys that could take her out and spend money on her. However, most of them turned out to be living on the edge, drug dealers.

The tears start to sting her face and Rick reaches out to her with a tissue in hand. She can't help but feel like he is such a blessing in her life. He came at the perfect time when she needed rescuing. She was tired of all the men she had met that were not worth her time. She needed a change and here he is, right beside her. She hears that voice inside her say, *Thank you, Lord.*

She looks around thinking Jazzman said those words but when she realizes it's her own thoughts, she is stunned. Did she really just talk to God? Maybe things are changing for her. So she does the unthinkable as she rests her head on Ricks shoulder needing his strong arms to protect her from her pain.

Rick senses what she needs. When around her, he is overcome with a need to be the man in her life to protect her. There is no hidden agenda with Kim, she is who she is and he is feelin' her.

The way they seem to know what the other is thinking is a connection that scares them both because they have spent such little time with one another. She is a beautiful story hidden in the rows of shelves at a bookstore, waiting to be discovered. He has found her and he is not letting her go.

Little did she know that Rick needs her just as much as she needs him, for his life has not been a walk in the park, but like most men he is not ready to disclose his trials and tribulations. The right moment will have to present itself to reveal the story he carries within. As he sits there watching the play, the tale being told is stirring up repressed memories of his own childhood. Still, the question on his mind is whether Kim will accept him once she learns of his past.

The play went on to showcase the story of the Harlem community through poetry reading, music and skits. It demonstrated the drug dealers that capitalized on it, and the relentless killings over more control as the poet states:

Every street corner is up for keeps
I have no problem killing you for more credibility
I'm on top of the world with power over these streets

The drug dealers wanted more territory in their possession, to gain more cash flow, to maintain that 'fruitful' yet dangerous lifestyle, gaining more authority in the streets by putting important people on their payroll. Their 'A List' consisted of cops and politicians in order to get the drugs into the city...the poet continues:

Hell...maybe I just watch too much TV
Watching cowboys and Indians fighting over territory
Do you think I'm so much different...No I don't think that really
My ass is just repeating the history that was taught to me
What the US Embassy dictates to the other countries
It's what I'm doing in the city
If you do not agree with my policy
I'll take your ass to war and claim my victory

To take down other drug dealers, there were the snitches and the crooked judges. Also on their payroll were garbage men and waste management owners in order to dispose of the bodies. It was a vicious cycle that had some people scared to leave their homes. Yet those who did knew what waited outside their front door.

Hell in the streets
How will I survive?
Harlem is me
I am the streets

Nevertheless one's love for the music had a way of sugar-coating the desperation to leave their neighborhood behind. The music sold you on the coolness of being part of the street. Selling drugs would give you power and exposing skin for sexual pleasure was a fashion statement:

I'll make moves on your girl if she is feeling me
I will have her sending your dumb ass to the penitentiary
So she can suck my ----
She can't help but want a brother like me

Yet, the vicious cycle of a drug dealer, staying on top of the world was also filled with fear of who would be the one to take it from them. Or, if they end up in jail who would be there to take over.

Hell, I blame the streets for why I'm so mean
I can't say I know my own family
It's funny 'cause my mom talks so much shit and judges me
But she has no problem taking money from me
You wanna know what's got me stuck on madness?
I got caught, now I lose years and time from living life free
And my own peeps already forgot about me
I took care of them fools when I was king of the streets
Now look at me, I'm locked up doin' time while they pray for me

The poetry and the music in this play are tied to the storyline in beautiful, deep messages. You feel each piece of the story through the lyrics of the songs and the voices that sing them. There was no escaping the emotions felt; the audience hungered for the next scene and they want to escape through the back doors of the brownstones on those streets of Harlem just like the actors. The audience wants to scream and shout the lyrics, "Harlem is ME, I AM the streets." During those times, even though people wanted to leave Harlem they stayed because of the music that lived in each of them. It was music that nurtured their soul and preached the message in overcoming trials and tribulations.

As the play ends and the lights gradually turn on, there were few dry eyes in the house. Some young men try to hide it, yet older men were not afraid to show the pain because they lived through those times in New York. Those men overcame the struggle and did not hide behind the macho mask. Those who faced those struggles in life related to this play, even Kim and Rick.

NEW YORK CITY, NY
Kim and Rick

Kim and Rick go out for drinks after the play to discuss their experience and interpretation of the play. They uncover some striking similarities with struggles growing up. Rick only tells her about being born to a woman who is addicted to drugs, how he has tried to save his mother time and time again, but she is too lost in the addiction to see her way out to a cleaner life. Rick admits his jealousy since drugs are her 'baby' and he has wanted to hold that title in her life. He concludes by telling her he has not been able to reach that goal.

After Rick briefly exposes his relationship with his mother, he asks, "So what had you crying at the beginning of the play?"

Kim is not sure how much to expose. She decides to test the waters and see how much he can handle before he starts to cringe. "Well…my mom…growing up I saw countless men in and out of our apartment. She would leave me with all sorts of people while she went out to the clubs. I witnessed her being abused emotionally and physically by men. I hated it. I saw this time and time again. In my mind I started to believe it was how a man showed a woman he truly loved her. Things would get so heated in my house, sometimes I would have Jazzman come over so I wouldn't have to hear the noise and the arguing in the other room. When it got really bad, I escaped to her house. I was scared and I hated the way they were hurting her and hurting me by hurting her."

She let her story end there, unwilling to share deeper haunting moments from her past with Rick. It feels too soon. Before Kim knew it, she is crying, yet the tears were not about the information she shared, but rather about the information she is holding back. To mask those details, she shifts gears. "I can't believe that…that was my reality…and my sanity was Jazzman. She helped me through some difficult times in my life. I have always wished to repay her for how she stood by my side for so many years and never judged me. When her mom passed away I felt helpless as a friend. I thought it was my moment to help her and many days I felt like I had no clue what to say or do to help her. I also feel so helpless when she has a bad day now. In those moments, I know she wishes she could talk to her mother, but she can't. She has meant so much to me. I want to see her happy and…I'm sorry I'm blabbing."

Rick pulls his chair to her side of the table. He senses that something else is going on with her from the way she shifted topics. He places a kiss on her forehead. "I hear you, but that would not be life. Life is about the cards we are dealt and how we go about resolving those issues internally. Our past experiences make us who we are and shape our character. Life has its ups and downs, so we have to make the most of it. We change it by accepting the things we can not change, but putting a positive spin on the situation to make it manageable."

Kim smiles, "So true, but bear with me I'm not there yet. Well, I do have another situation. I'M TIRED."

"Say no more! Let's go home." Rick gets up and reaches for Kim's hand.

Hearing those words felt good. It helps her feel secure. From the moment she met Rick, in a weird way she feels in his presence that she is in good hands. For the first time she feels wanted and it feels good. However, she fears these feelings. It seems foreign to her experiences in life. She fears that she might push him away with negative self-talk by believing that she is not worthy. She convinces herself, *One day at a time, Kim. One day at a time. Get to know the feeling before you push it away. Learn to put an end to heartache and welcome joy. You deserve it.*

It would seem that making love would spoil what they discovered tonight, but instead it made their connection stronger. It is a moment in time, an injection filled with strong passion, a kiss that turns a vulnerable person into a confident one with a secure state of mind. With each touch, it feels like years of celibacy finally unleashed. Their lovemaking fills the space with every heightened need and desire. Each plateau of excitement leads to deeper emotions, a release of pent-up tension that has been building in them for their whole lives. Two souls who have struggled, finally find someone they connect with on so many levels that words are unable to capture what their passion has uncovered.

Kim cries out, "Touch me softly...don't stop...I need you."

Rick overcomes her insecurities by expressing, "I've got you...I'm not letting you go...You are where you belong...right here with me in my arms."

As he reaches for a condom and finds his way to move slowly inside her, she inhales for some air. A feeling filled her heart with security, excitement of perhaps a love she has never felt, but always knew existed. He has left her open to the possibility of a long-term commitment, a feeling she thought would never surface in her life. Her arms wrap around his caramel, rock-solid body. It fits like a glove shielding her from the cold world. His skin against her naked flesh feels tender to her touch. Together they are a perfect fit. Kim laces her hands around the back of his neck and looks into his eyes declaring, "You...feel...so...good!" Kim's fantasies of being with him did not do this moment any justice.

Their bodies lock into place as they rock slowly at a perfect pace. The rhythm brings them to unite as one and their moans are enough to put them over the edge. Their souls have connection binding them. It feels like they are finally where they are meant to be, and a part of them knows deep down there is no turning back.

Chapter 4

MIAMI, FL

Jazzman's Journal

Dear Mom:

I was going through some old boxes and found a poem I wrote about daddy and you, years after he left us. I needed some closure on what he did to us so I expressed it through what comes natural to me, poetry. I never shared this with you, so here it is:

Just when she thought she had it all
Just one thing ruined it all
The pain inflicted by the one she loved
When she said, "I Do"
She had no idea it would turn out this way

What did she do?
What did she say?
That would make you react in anger
And hit her that way
You're hurting her and she has no say
All she knows is that she lives in your house
And she must obey

In one corner of the room
Blocking herself away from you
She can only cry and hope
The pain will one day go away
She is suffering inside
Because of the abuse she can no longer bear
She is like a running faucet
A stream of blood not of water
Yell or scream
But do not hit her again
Her body can only take so much
She wants to leave, but where can she go?
She has no other place to call her home

There is only one thing left for her to do
As she cries out in anger and frustration
She says,
"Please hit me once more
I will have you locked up and throw away the key!
Maybe then you will realize what you have done
DO NOT SAY YOU'RE SORRY!
Because I won't fall for it anymore
Just stay out of my life so I can wed once more
But with a man who has respect
That will give me the love and courage
To start my life all over again."

Reading this poem brought back haunting memories of you sending me to Kim's house for sleepovers. I would argue with you because I wanted to stay. I could not bear to leave you at home with daddy. I wanted to help you, protect you, but you tried to protect me from the truth. Only, I already knew the truth…daddy was an abuser and I hated what he did to you. I knew, mommy, and I'm so sorry you had to go through that traumatic experience alone. I never brought it up because I know how much it hurt you. I know that was not the life you wanted for me. In a way, I wish we had talked about it because I have this void with your passing. Somewhere inside of me, I feel that because we did not discuss daddy's leaving, I can't make peace with our past.

Mommy, I'm glad I got to tell you right before you closed your eyes that one of my dreams is to open up a shelter for battered women. I remember when I said to you, "it will serve as a home for the women who need a place of refuge from a life of verbal and physical abuse." You smiled. I remember how your face lit up when you heard about the motivational classes, the literature courses, the counseling and the transitional living space…all designed to empower them to be confident women. It's a moment that I will never forget.

I love you and I miss you. I have to go for now, I'm going away with Afrique. We need some quality time because he's been on tour. I can't wait to tell you all about it when I get back. I'm glad that my therapist suggested writing to you. She said it might help and so far it feels good. I know you want me to heal. Please continue to watch over me.

'TIL WE MEET AGAIN WITH A SUNSET!!!

~ Love, Jazzman~

Jazzman brushes back her long brown hair, and closes the journal as her emotions get the best of her. She grabs a tissue from her nightstand to wipe away the tears that are welling up in her eyes. She takes a deep breath and when she exhales, she feels a weight lift off her shoulders from releasing some of the feelings she held inside. Gaining some energy, she grabs her luggage from the closet and begins to pack for her weekend getaway to Cabo San Lucas, Mexico. She has heard great things from her friends in the entertainment industry that have vacationed there. She is excited to finally visit.

She packs light with shorts, revealing tops, sexy dresses and sandals. Her stilettos are a must. She selects clothing that will accentuate and reveal her curves, a body that she works hard to maintain.

She doesn't need to pack her bikini because she will get that on-site. It's become a tradition for Afrique to have a new one waiting for her when she opens the door to the hotel room. It's a personal joke between them from the first night they spent together in Miami, when Jazzman did not have a fresh pair of underwear to wear the next morning. He had to guess her butt size. Now, to make up for thinking she needed a large due to her physique, he buys her a tiny bikini every time they vacation, in apology.

Jazzman is always excited to see him, but this time feels different in part because she is somewhat disappointed in herself. When she accepted the invitation from Afrique, she didn't think she would still be working on the music video. All that was left to do was editing, but she likes to follow through and finish her work. She is feeling uneasy about delegating the editing work just to have personal time with Afrique. Jazzman brushes it off saying to herself that he is the man she is going to marry and some sacrifices have to be made in order for the relationship to stay solid.

As Jazzman packs her clothes neatly into the luggage, she smiles remembering their last getaway to a place she had always dreamed of visiting, Hawaii. She laughs at how Maui was supposed to be an overnight stay for snorkeling, but the beaches were as she put it, "so freakin' breathtaking" that Afrique extended their stay on that island.

As she folds several more pieces of clothing into the suitcase she giggles at what he said, "We have more time on this amazing island because there is a beautiful woman here who has the most incredible sparkle in her eye and she smiled at me. I think I'm falling in love with her. This woman has the potential of being your competition…you better watch out Jazzman."

During that trip Jazzman realized there was much more to life and it came from nature. Her desire to go to Oahu for shopping had seemed of less importance while on Maui. So when they finally made their way to the other island, her urge to go shopping surfaced once again, but only as a reaction to an argument with Afrique and their living arrangements. He suggested that they move to Jamaica, which sounded completely crazy to her. The part she was most upset about was that he suggested it knowing her whole career is based out of Miami and that her plans included maybe one day even moving to New York or Los Angeles. Since he didn't back down, she told him she would think about it and was miserable from the moment she said it.

Jazzman lets out a sigh and says to herself, *This trip will be different…Positive thoughts, Jazzman. Positive thoughts.*

Jazzman is still feeling upset as she remembers that day, so she tries to forget by tidying up her room, but she can't. She remembers feeling so alone on a beautiful island and not having Kim or Tyson to talk to about her feelings. So to get her mind off the situation she did what Kim would recommend, go shopping. Then she went for a walk, something Tyson would do with her. When she did, she was able to appreciate the beautiful island of Oahu. As a creative person that memory was priceless. The best part was that she learned how to control her emotions by going for a walk that day. She has gone for walks many times since then to relieve herself from the stress she feels.

Her feelings of frustration subside as she remembers Afrique finally coming to his senses and understanding her point of view concerning their move to Jamaica. She remembers how they made up by going out for drinks and dancing. Jazzman thought as many others do, that Limbo dancing was Hawaiian dancing. However Afrique schooled her that Limbo dancing originated in Trinidad.

The night ended on a very positive note for Jazzman as the 'Hawaiian' Hula music caused her to move her body seductively in slow circular motions, her hips swaying from side to side. She remembers how her movements turned him on, bringing him to the dance floor. He pulled her tight against his body to finish the dance with her. She felt his excitement and it fueled her own desires. Each movement on the dance floor increased their level of passion, so the rest of the evening was spent finding creative ways of making up.

Apart from that misunderstanding, the remainder of the trip was quite romantic. On that trip they learned they don't have to agree all the time. Still, they learned to put their differences aside in order to enjoy each other's company and have a good time. It's a trip that brought mixed emotions and strengthened their love for one another.

∽◌

CABO SAN LUCAS, MEXICO
Jazzman and Afrique

"Wow!" Jazzman exclaims as she opens the door to the villa on the beach. She already expects this to be a long, romantic weekend, but just when it seems Afrique's romantic gestures can't get any better he out does himself again.

She finds her way into the bedroom, and on the bed is a bikini, flowers and a note. She giggles in excitement as she reads:

If I had one day left on this earth,
I'd spend it with you.
I would inhale the air you breathe,
So I may always remember,
The woman who continuously takes my breath away.

The note, the villa's breathtaking view, the romantic aura, all help to calm the uneasy feelings she was having about Afrique. It also helps her to not be so hard on herself for leaving unfinished business at the record label. She needed a break from working so hard. The villa is extravagant - the type of place that brothers get while on vacation just to make sure they 'get some'. This would be the spot that would make a woman's panties drop and ask, 'how do you want it?' The room's décor is inviting with rich ruby, violet, mauve and burgundy tones. The curvy chairs, sofas and flowing drapes bring out an exotic energy. The candles were lit for her arrival and it's exactly what she needs to help her leave the stress behind and focus on her man.

An hour later, Afrique walks in, happy to see Jazzman, who is rubbing lotion on her already smooth body. He loves the moment of seeing her after being away from her, whether it's been a few days or weeks. Immediately, he greets her with a tight squeeze and allows his lips to reunite with hers. He takes a moment to taste her neck and whispers, "I missed you."

She exhales in excitement and whispers back, "I missed you, too."

He holds her at arm's length, "How was your flight?"

She smiles and gives him a look, "Good since it was bringing me to you."

He smiles, "You must want something."

She giggles, "Of course." She hands him the lotion, "Care to work your magic?"

"I thought you'd never ask." He takes over as he reapplies the lotion on her legs and works his hands up to her thighs.

His touch makes her weak. He feeds off her energy and intensifies the mood. He allows his tongue to explore other parts of her body, teasing her midsection. After rediscovering familiar territory, he comes up for air and expresses, "I missed your beautiful body. You are so damn sexy."

She smiles, "I missed you too, baby."

He plays with her some more, teasing her as he works his hands up to her beautifully exposed breasts, massaging each one, feeling them on his lips, fulfilling her needs.

She lets it be known, "I need you."

He obliges by tantalizing her, allowing the intensity to grow before gliding inside her.

She screams, "Damn, you feel so good!" She caresses his back pressing his body against hers as he injects her body with pleasure. Their heat rises as he goes deeper, deeper than he has ever been inside her.

He uses all his willpower to stop for a moment and allow their desires of wanting to grow. His mouth finds its way to her nipple and he bites it making her scream. Her body is exposed to unfamiliar pain and she is enjoying every moment of it. Her moans drive him insane knowing he is doing her body some much needed justice.

She begs, "Please, baby, come back inside. I've missed you."

That is all he needs to hear. He allows her to feel him again, and it's apparent in their touch that they are way overdue. This time he isn't coming out until her body explodes from satisfaction.

✎

CABO SAN LUCAS, MEXICO
Jazzman and Afrique

"Surprise!" The next morning Afrique takes Jazzman to a secluded part of the villa where the terrace overlooks an infinity pool. Their terrace has a dressed bed with emerald, aqua, sapphire and indigo colors from the sheets to the pillows to the canapé drapes. The bed is right by the ocean and to her surprise it is set up for a private photo shoot - photos of her just for Afrique's enjoyment. Now, she understands why the bikini he picked for her on this trip was white and elegant.

Jazzman expresses, "Baby, this is so beautiful and so romantic. You have completely out done yourself."

Afrique wraps his arm around her waist and pulls her close to him. "With you these things just come naturally. I love you, Jazz, and I can't wait to spend the rest of my life with you."

She presses her lips against his and then looks into his eyes, "I can't wait for you to be my husband so I can ask you to grab the remote for me while I make you watch the girly shows with me."

They both start laughing.

Afrique corrects her, "I think neither one of us will be getting the remote. That's what kids are for. They need order and discipline, right?"

"Of course, but I would still want you to get the remote for me so I can admire your body from a distance." Jazzman says seductively as she drops her robe to the floor and stands before Afrique in the two-piece bikini.

"Damn, Jazz..." Afrique rubs his manhood trying to stroke it down because he wants to get through this photo shoot. "...You have a way with words. I want to slowly lay you on that bed and make love to you." He rubs his manhood against her mid section.

The touch gets her excited and her juices flowing. "So, what are you going to do about it? Take a rain check on the photo shoot and let our bodies merge into one? Or do you want pictures of all this so you can fantasize when you are on tour?"

Afrique tries to regain his composure and says, "Let's stick to the agenda. I need these photos of you when you are not around to please me. But I promise you we will come back out here later to finish what you started."

A part of Jazzman is a bit disappointed with his answer. "Okay, where do you want me?"

"On the bed—"

They both look at each other and bust out laughing recognizing the unintended double meaning behind those words. Their laughter helps alter the mood and let them get down to the business of the photo shoot.

Jazzman is not used to being on the other side of the camera. She feels paralyzed about what to do, but with some guidance from Afrique she begins warming up to the camera. He instructs her on where to place her arms, how to position her legs and what to do with the placement of her head. He even shouts out what expression he wants her to convey and as more shots are taken, her professional experience takes over in terms of what she needs to do for the perfect shot.

As Afrique snaps away, he photographs her well-shaped curves for personal pleasure. He captures what a man desires as he turns the pages of a magazine full of beautiful women. The sex appeal is obvious in each freeze frame, the way her butt is popping out, the way her breasts are full and the way her facial expressions tell a man he is wanted. Jazzman's body is perfectly curved for what he wants to capture in a photograph.

What she would discover later on, is the shots that felt awkward to her were some of her best shots and the ones she thought would turn out fabulous were not as natural. It is a great learning experience for her and it will help her with her upcoming directing gigs.

After the photo shoot Afrique and Jazzman enjoy a breakfast on the terrace on elegant white china with 14K gold trimming. The crystal glasses are casting beautiful reflections of the sun's rays.

The moment makes Jazzman pinch herself which she did from time to time when she is in awe of her own good fortune and lifestyle. It's also what makes her question internally, *am I ready for all this?* As she thinks these words she realizes they are Tyson's words. It's what he asked her when she first showed him her engagement ring. She remembers something else Tyson said, "You'll be taking a huge step into a lifetime commitment." When he said that, she felt as if a rock was hitting her right in the stomach. Her harsh reality is facing a long-term commitment with Afrique and it has her stuck. Even though she has a great deal of love for him, she still has doubts. Her main one - will their lifestyles be able to withstand a marriage? He's a famous musician with many women desiring him and many will resent her place by his side.

She begins to consider some very harsh realities. *I understand the lifestyle fairly well, but is this something I want for myself? The women who throw themselves at him, may become a little too much for me to handle. I thought I could handle it, but now that I'm in it, it's different. It's an intense ball game. Is it right for me to question his lifestyle? When my exes used to give me lip about my relationships in the industry I was quick to cut them off...I wasn't risking my career for a man's insecurity. Now, I feel like a hypocrite. I should be able to handle this and I'm not sure I can. How can something I love so much, music, be the very same thing that I hate, when it comes to the man I love.*

Afrique calls out, "Jazzman where are you? What's on your mind?"

56

Jazzman snaps out of her dream-like trance, "I'm sorry, I was just thinking about work." Jazzman stuffs her mouth with a bite of omelet and a piece of toast to prevent herself from saying too much.

Afrique senses something and says, "That's it? Is everything okay?"

Jazzman responds, "Yes, nothing I can't handle." She takes a sip of coffee not knowing what to say next.

"Do you need to talk about it? You know I'm a great listener." Afrique senses a change and he is concerned, wondering if something is wrong.

"No, I'm good. I'm still trying to sort everything in my mind. I'm not sure how to process it all but when I do…and if I need someone to bounce it off of…I will come to you." She smiles and takes another bite of her food.

He says jokingly, "Use me and abuse me, is that all I'm good for? Man, I thought I meant more to you than that." Although a part of him is still wondering what she seems worried about.

"You know I love you. You mean the world to me. It's work and something about my childhood that I'm still processing. I don't have all the pieces. So I'm still trying to figure it all out before I ask for advice. I hope you can understand."

"I do." He holds her hand.

"Hey, I thought you had a surprise for me?" She says this rubbing his hand hoping he understands that she wants to change the subject.

"I do, but it arrives tomorrow. That reminds me, I have to get going if I want to surprise you with your gift before you leave."

Jazzman grows sad, "Oh, you're leaving me?"

"Yes, my love."

Jazzman gives him a sad look. "No, don't go."

Afrique gives her the same look. "I CAN stay but you won't get your surprise, darling. Besides you'll have some time to yourself to think of whatever it is that's on your mind."

She can sense his attitude, "O—kay…" She sits on his lap to comfort him and wraps her arms around him. "…I'll miss you and I will be ready for you when you get back. I'll be dressed to kill, with little on…just the way you like it!"

"Mmm, sounds good to me." Afrique gently smacks her ass. "Just make sure you have on a pair of stilettos."

Jazzman replies, "I'll make it hot, *papi*," she kisses him on the lips.

As Afrique walks out the door, Jazzman feels that he senses she is not being completely honest with him. She feels bad about that, but she needs to figure this out on her own. She believes the only way to accomplish this is by talking it out through therapy. She does not want her feelings to get fogged by someone else's agenda. This way she is pleasing her needs and not someone else's needs.

Since Jazzman has some time to herself she goes for a walk along the beach to clear her mind. The more she questions herself, the more she walks and before she knows it she's walked several miles. During that walk, she realizes she is angry with herself for not staying and finishing the music video job. Although she loves her time with Afrique, she feels like she abandoned her own goals to fulfill her man's needs. She has seen so many people get together and break up in the music industry. She worries about her chances of lasting with Afrique. She has yet to reach her own personal goals in life. So giving up a piece of herself for a man makes her question, *something isn't sitting right? I can't wait to go to therapy. I really need to ask myself some hard questions. I need answers. I'm scared, but I have to face my fears. I have to uncover this feeling at the pit of my stomach. Help me Lord. Help me find my way.*

CABO SAN LUCAS, MEXICO
Jazzman and Afrique

"Surprise!" Afrique moves his hands away from covering Jazzman's eyes. She is definitely surprised by the portraits that surround her. All the images are of her. It's a little weird, and she's unsure what to do with all of them.

"These are beautiful." She picks up one of the nineteen by thirty-eight landscape portraits of her kneeling on the bed with a beautiful view of the ocean behind her. "I can't believe this is me. I look so beautiful in this picture. You are an amazing photographer."

"It's easy when the model is flawless. You are a natural beauty." He kisses her on the cheek.

"Thank you. I love them all. You did an amazing job with this. I don't know what to say."

"You don't have to say anything but tease me and please me. That was the deal. You told me you were going to drop it like it's hot. I'm waiting." Afrique smiles and slips his tongue teasingly into her savoring mouth.

She pulls away batting her eyes, "Really, I said that? The only thing I recall is telling you I will tie you to the bed and do WHATEVER I want to you."

"You are crazy...but I think...it would be better if I do that to you."

"What's wrong, you don't trust me to untie you? I promise to do so when I'm done." She whispers in his ear, "Using my mouth to touch you in all the right places..."

"I think I would get much more pleasure if you were tied up and I could touch you in all the right places without any interruptions." He pulls her close to unbutton her shorts. "Then when the sensation is too much I promise to stop and travel to another part of your body." He gently kisses her neck and whispers, "Making you so freakin' wet that you will want me to finish the job inside you. Are you down?"

Before any tying could take place they are wrapped in each other's arms pleasing and teasing. They are enjoying what the other has to offer by bringing to life their pleasure points. It's a moment of satisfaction to carry them through until the next time they reunite as lovers.

Chapter 5

MIAMI, FL
Jazzman

Jazzman gets back from her weekend trip with Afrique and there are several voicemail messages from her boss. The initial messages seem urgent, but the last one indicates he is all set. Hearing all those messages brings on an uncomfortable feeling in the pit of her stomach. She feels like crap for not being in town to accept his calls.

She looks at the time. It is too late to call Tyson, and she drives herself crazy with thoughts wondering what is so urgent that her boss is calling her at home. The biggest question, what price will she have to pay for missing his calls.

In order to fall asleep she tries to tell herself that the calls were not important, but she knows that Charles does not call on the weekends unless it is very important. Whatever the case, she hopes she is not in trouble for leaving her work in the hands of a co-worker and not being accessible.

MIAMI, FL

Tyson and Charles (Jazzman's Boss)

Tyson knocks on the door to his boss's office.

Charles calls out, "Come in."

Tyson asks, "You wanted to see me?"

Charles still looking at his computer answers, "Yes, take a seat. Let me just finish this email."

Tyson waits calmly, wondering what this is all about, as Charles finishes typing.

Charles looks over at Tyson, "I want to run something by you before I recommend you for the job."

Tyson is curious, "Talk to me."

Charles continues, "We are looking to expand our distribution. We have a deal on the table in New York and I need someone in the city for six months to a year to head the operation. I'm tied up down here, but I think you would be perfect for the job. You proved that this weekend. Our business partners in New York gave me remarkable feedback on your presentation. You've been putting in your time. It's been noticed and I think you are definitely the man for the job. I can count on you. I know it would be a huge adjustment, but I think this would be an excellent opportunity for you. What do you think? Is this something you want to pursue? Do you want some time to think about it?"

Tyson tries to hide his excitement and calmly answers, "There is nothing to think about. I've been waiting for an opportunity like this. I'm game. Thank you. I appreciate this."

Charles replies, "It's a no brainer. But, I must warn you…life in New York is no joke. There are a lot of sharks up north. You also have to put in long hours at the office and it is a fast paced life. You'll need to attend showcases in New York to expand on our Hip Hop label. I'll need you to head that up for us. Also, the artists that you feel have strong potential, you'll need to sell them a dream and once you have that signature your work is just beginning. You will be putting in long hours at the studio making sure we have some money-making songs. This is a whole differ- ent ball game. In New York you will be rollin' with the big dogs. So don't look at this as an easy ride. You have a long road ahead of you, but I know you will adapt to the lifestyle. You have swag and you'll blend in. I'm going to have a couple of my people groom you for the job."

Tyson smiles, "No doubt. I got this. This is my specialty. Get those guys in the club, hire a few women to mess with their heads and get them fired up. Sell them a dream by showing them what life will be like if they sign on the dotted line. I got this!"

They both laugh. Charles pulls out two Cuban cigars from his drawer and lights them up as they further discuss the details of the New York position.

∽๑

MIAMI, FL
Jazzman and Tyson

[Knock! Knock!]

Jazzman shouts out, "Come in."

Tyson opens the door to Jazzman's office and loves the music she is listening to, The Temptations. It's like she knew. The song "I know, I'm Losing You" is exactly the way he's feeling knowing his move to New York will put a huge wedge in their relationship. "Hey beautiful, how are you?"

Jazzman's face lights up as she answers, "I'm good and you?"

Internally Tyson already feels awkward, "I'm good. I have some good news to share with you."

Jazzman puts her pen down to give him her undivided attention, "Oh, did you have a hot date last night?"

Tyson is not really thrilled with her response, "No, nothing like that. I just got offered a job in New York and I accepted the position." He left a little suspense in his response to see how she will react.

Jazzman expresses sadness and it appears that she almost wants to cry, "What…what are you talking about? I thought you were happy here. Leave Miami, are you sure you want to do this?"

"I'm sure."

"I'm lost…I didn't see this coming. Which label? What will you be doing? I had no idea. Have I been so engrossed in my own life that I wasn't being a friend to you? I don't get it, I'm puzzled."

Tyson has been feeling a little lonely and missing her closeness, her friendship. So to hear her react this way makes him happy that she still cares. "It's not like that. Charles offered me a job in NYC and I accepted the offer. He wants me there for six months to about a year."

It finally hits Jazzman that the calls placed to her home this past weekend were a big deal, but just to confirm her suspicion she questions, "When did this come about? What did I miss while I was away?"

Tyson appears disappointed in her response, especially knowing this could have been her gig. "Well, Charles needed you in New York this past weekend. When he did not get a hold of you he asked me and I jumped on the first flight out. He is expanding on the record label. He wants me to head the distribution deal that's in the works. He has a couple of deals on the table, but he is still ironing it out. He also wants me to scout new talent for our new Hip Hop division."

Jazzman can't believe what she missed. "Wow!"

"Well, are you going to congratulate your boy or what?"

Jazzman is stunned. She is upset finding herself missing out on an opportunity due to her relationship. However, she gets up from behind her desk to give Tyson a tight squeeze. "Of course. Congrats! I'm so proud of you. I have to confess I don't want you to go. I'm going to miss you. I'm not going to be able to bug you whenever I want. We can't go for walks or have lunch together. I'm not going to see your handsome face in the morning. This is not cool." The whole time she is talking they are lost in the moment, finding that they are still holding one another. They pull away, each a little reluctant to end the embrace feeling a temptation to share a kiss.

For just one second, Tyson imagines getting on his knees and asking her to join him in New York, as silly as he knows that would sound. He wishes she could move with him and they could be two souls getting to know unfamiliar territory. "I'm going to miss you too, Jazz."

Jazzman is scared to ask, "When are you leaving me? I mean... when are you leaving?"

Tyson laughs to himself answering, "I'm leaving in about a month, but it could be sooner. You know how that goes. Charles mentioned that I will be living in Brooklyn, my old hometown."

Jazzman laughs, "Does it qualify as your hometown if you left when you were a toddler?"

Tyson smiles and his pearly whites are exposed. "New York is in my blood. It's never left me. When I've gone back to visit my cousins I feel like I belong there. I'm not crazy about those brutal winters and terrible beaches. Yet, I feel like it's meant for me to be in the city and this is my chance. It's going to feel good. I'm glad I got family there...A man needs to eat and I will be hitting up my aunts for some home cooked meals."

"Hey, you can probably hang out with Rick."

Tyson looks puzzled, "Who the hell is Rick?"

Jazzman laughs, "Rick...Kim's friend or boyfriend."

"Oh that Rick. The girl goes through men like she goes through panties."

Jazzman turns beet red, "Hey, that's not nice and that's a false statement. Watch how you talk about my girl. Besides, he's really helped tame her ways. I'm not sure of their status, but I'm pretty sure he's her man by now. They hit it off from the moment they met."

"I bet they hit IT."

Jazzman shakes her head and rolls her eyes simultaneously. "Anyways, I'm just worried about the distance between them. You know how long-distance relationships can turn out." Jazzman feels embarrassed, realizing she just put her foot in her mouth.

Tyson picks up on it and confirms, "Look who's calling the kettle black."

"Yes, I think you've made your point. I do have my own drama." She tries to justify it, adding, "At least I'm engaged and it won't stay this way forever."

Tyson responds, "Have you two decided where you are going to live? He's an artist who is on the road all the time, Jazz. It ain't gonna change. Or are you still in denial? It will be a part of your life. If you haven't accepted that yet, word to the wise - you need to start. Once again I question, do you really know what you're getting yourself into?"

Again she turns beet red not expecting the conversation to turn to what she has been questioning for the last several weeks. "Let's not do this right now, Tyson."

He responds, "Whatever, Jazz. You need to start looking at it because I don't know if I can be the one to pick up the pieces of your broken heart. This might sting a little, but news flash, I'm leaving to New York. I'm not going to be here for you every time things fall apart for you with another man. I wish you would see that I need you, too."

Not sure of what to say, but for the sake of saying something she asks, "What do you want from me?"

"You know what I want. Deep down inside you...you know you want it too. Don't take this as I'm saying I've had enough of us. I'm saying it because I need you to open up your eyes. Like I've told you before, marriage is a huge step and I don't think you need to commit yourself to someone so soon. You have your whole life ahead of you. You are letting this man dictate your future. You are losing the essence of Jazzman to a man. You need to check yourself before you get lost and later down the road wonder what happened to you. You have an amazing mind and the ability to do many great things. Don't get lost. I know you want love. You deserve it, but not like this when your hustle is just beginning. I worry because I know what you are capable of achieving. Don't lose yourself...find yourself." Tyson feels satisfied with getting that off his chest.

Jazzman is dumfounded, "Damn...wow...tell me how you really feel." Her tears sting her eyes, but she tries to hold them back. "Did you have to lay it on me like that? News flash, I have been doing some soul-searching. I'm not sure where that road will take me, but stay tuned."

Tyson responds nearly whispering, "I'm sorry, but I'm tired of the games. I'm at a different place in my life and I wouldn't be a friend if I sugarcoat the truth. I'm sorry baby girl, but it is what it is. You need to realize that you are not ready for marriage. Hey, why don't you try therapy? If you are scared and need a friend, I can go with. I can be your support system. Tell me what you need, I got you."

Jazzman looks into his eyes, recognizing the feelings behind his words. She gets sad, remembering he will soon be leaving to New York. "Actually, I've gone. I was nervous at first, but it turned out to be very insightful. I've only had my first session, but I think it will help me. There is a lot I've buried deep down inside me. I just pray that I learn something from the visits. I hope it doesn't turn out to be a waste of time."

"Nothing ventured..."

"Nothing gained."

Tyson's curious, "Why didn't you tell me? I'm happy for you, Jazz. That is a huge step."

"Like you said...I need to figure out some things. I'm trying to get some answers to things that have my emotions all screwed up. I want to get past some old wounds and grow. However, I need to do this on my own and that's the reason why I haven't said anything." Jazzman feels proud of her decision to go to therapy.

Tyson is happy for her. "Well while you go through this process I want you to hang onto a scripture that will hopefully put things into perspective for you. Mark 4:25...to those who have, more will be given—"

Jazzman looks startled, then thoughtful. "I know that one."

Tyson continues, "—Well, I don't know if you know the meaning behind it, but you still have a lot of self-fulfilling to proclaim. You are not done growing, if you become a wife, now, you will lose a part of yourself. You are a good woman and if you get married you will put your husband's needs first. Given where you are right now, you need to put yourself first. I don't want you to end up being just another housewife. You have so much to offer. 'Cause if you don't do 'YOU' first…remember the ending part of that scripture…from those who have nothing, even what they have will be taken away. To me that means when you don't shoot for the stars, when you don't fulfill your own desires you may end up lost and lose your way."

Jazzman is enlightened by his words of wisdom. His message helps her to see something she has been struggling with for a while. But she bites her bottom lip not wanting to say too much, at least not right now. "Thank you. When I'm confused or lost I will remember that scripture." She loves the way he connects with her spirit. Briefly, she wonders if God is sending her a message.

Tyson smiles, "Good, I'm glad you're going to therapy. If you need to talk…I'm here. By the way, I might plan a vacation before leaving to New York."

"Where are you going?"

"New Orleans for the Jazz festival…I think it will be a nice treat to listen to good music before the long hours in the city take over."

"Actually, I'm putting together a proposal for Charles on expanding our markets with Jazz and Latino music. If approved, I think you and I should go to New Orleans together and start looking at prospects. We can expense it and make it your farewell between friends. What do you say?"

Tyson, getting excited, responds, "Sounds like a plan to me!"

"Good…Now that I put my goal out there in the universe…I need to get moving on it. Let me get my butt into gear."

"Same here…I have a lot on my plate. I'm going to head back to my office."

Jazzman lets out a small laugh. "By the way, I won't be able to do lunch today. I have Oriba in the studio and I'm going to join him."

"Cool! Tell him I said what's up." Tyson kisses her on the forehead and walks out.

⌀

MIAMI, FL
Jazzman

Once again, Jazzman finds herself nervous as she heads into therapy for the second time. She has been more prone to headaches since her first session, maybe due to all the concerns that have clouded her mind. One of those concerns...will therapy work? She feels like it will, but a part of her still doubts the process, since Kim has gone to numerous sessions with no success at all. However, she is fascinated that since beginning therapy, she has begun to ask the hard questions she failed to ask before and failed to ever address on her own. She hopes that self-discovery will begin to unfold before her eyes. She is nervous about the decisions she has to make, but she can't wait for the end result.

She questions, *or is there one? Is self-discovery an ongoing process? Does it end at a specific age or does it keep reinventing itself as time passes.*

When she enters the waiting room, her mood shifts, responding to the soft, therapeutic music that greets her, putting her at ease.

Helen calls out, "Jazzman?"

"Yes."

"Please come in. I'm just wrapping up some notes."

Jazzman walks into the office and sits on the sofa. Helen closes the manila folder, grabs another and turns to Jazzman, "How are you?"

Jazzman returns the smile, "I'm good. Yourself?"

"Busy, but good. Let me review and then we can get started." Helen opens up Jazzman's folder and reads quickly through her notes. "So, I gave you a homework assignment. Were you able to tackle it?"

Jazzman responds with excitement, "I did! I wrote to my mom and it felt good. It made me feel close to her. I needed to feel that

69

since she is the one I used to talk to all the time. It was therapeutic. Once my dad left, he was never a topic for discussion, so I talked to her about him in my journal. I was able to communicate my feelings about what happened when I was a kid. At the time, I was in pain, too. I did not like what he was doing to my mom. I was also able to see how she tried to protect me. I think her way of coping with that time in her life was to not bring it up. I think it was also to prevent herself from bad-mouthing my dad. There is a saying at the office, if you don't have anything good to say don't say anything at all."

Helen adds, "Yes, I agree."

Jazzman and Helen look at one another and smile.

Jazzman continues, "So, when my mom passed suddenly and unexpectedly, I didn't get the chance to talk to her about my dad. I didn't realize how much that bothered me and how much it was weighing on my mind. As I wrote in my journal it all became much clearer."

Helen asks, "How do you feel about your mom not talking to you about your dad?"

Jazzman thinks for a few seconds, "Well...I want to say...well...I don't think I'm mad, but I am sad...a little hurt...because I think... well, I feel I deserved more being that he was my dad. I still needed his love. The problems they had were their issues. I still needed a dad. Now, I'm in a relationship and I still feel broken inside. If I don't get a grip on what's going on internally, how am I going to give my all to another man?"

Helen answers, "Hmm. Are you supposed to give all of yourself to a man?"

Jazzman is puzzled by the question, knowing she will have to think about this some more. It was not what she expected to hear. "Interesting question. I never looked at it like that."

Helen smiles, "Think about that some more."

Jazzman also smiles, "I'm going to. Thank you! So, at this point I'm not sure how to get over my dad leaving when I was a little girl. Lately I've been asking myself if I am marriage material. I don't feel like it. You know, I get that every girl dreams about getting married and having a big wedding. But what good is it if the timing isn't right? I know that a lot of women dream of being in my position. I wonder if I am crazy for even questioning this wonderful man that I have in my life."

Helen responds with hesitation, "You know, Jazzman, sometimes our inner voice speaks to us and the questions you are asking yourself are very good questions. Some people avoid or ignore that voice inside. You are not crazy. Your inner voice is communicating with you. This will make more sense as we get deeper into these sessions."

Jazzman appears a little confused as Helen expected.

Jazzman continues, "Well, there is that other part of me that says I have a real shot at love here. I think I should roll with it and see where the road leads. He's an amazing guy and we understand one another. I'm at a crossroad and I need to figure out if I'm going left or right. So I wonder...should I continue the way I'm going and fine tune it or...I'm sorry, I don't know if I'm making any sense."

Helen responds peacefully, "You are doing fine, Jazzman. You don't have to apologize. Before we go any further, what is your fiancé's name?"

Jazzman answers, "Afrique."

Jazzman looks at Helen to see her response, wondering if she recognizes the name. When it appears that she doesn't and might actually be thinking to herself 'what an odd name', Jazzman continues, "He's a musician from Jamaica."

Helen asks, "Please tell me more about Afrique and what is making you have mixed feelings."

"Well, I work for a record label and I'm just beginning to move up the ladder. While my fiancé is already an established musician and he's been quite successful for some time. Since I'm just starting out, it's been hard for me to balance love and career. I recently began getting more directing jobs and that meant I was canceling some of our planned getaways. Then, I felt some resistance on his part and I thought he was starting to have a change of heart. So,

I started canceling some of my directing jobs to be with him and spend more quality time together. He became accustomed to me catering to his needs. I admit I enjoyed it, too. So now we basically plan our getaways according to his schedule. Which is fine, but I know I'm not established enough to give up job opportunities. So, I guess it really isn't 'fine', but I'm not sure where that leaves me and what that means for our relationship." Jazzman looks at Helen to see if she has any questions.

Helen emphasizes, "I see. Is that the only thing that concerns you about him?"

Jazzman answers, "No, there are several major things that happened prior to us getting engaged." Jazzman goes on to explain their one-night stand and how they lost touch after that night. She tells Helen how Afrique had not been upfront with her about two very important things in his life – having a son and his living arrangement with his son's mother.

After explaining those events, she continues, "I feel like I must add that Afrique said he started off as good friends with Jackie. One night their friendship grew intimate and Jackie ended up pregnant. From there they tried to continue the relationship, but it didn't work. So living in the same house for the sake of their son is what they decided to do."

Helen asks, "Would you say that Afrique has had a lot of one-night stands or a lot of spontaneous behavior without thinking of the consequences?"

Jazzman is intrigued by Helen's question. "I think so."

"How do you feel about that?"

Jazzman thinks for a moment, "Insecure. Case in point, we went away recently and I started really thinking about my relationship with him. I feel like our relationship is beginning to be more about him and what works for him. I feel like if I cancel my plans to meet up with him, that he might fall into another one-night stand and that thought terrifies me. However, when I arrive at these expensive getaways I ask myself, what's wrong with you, Jazz? Do you know how many women would die for this type of life and affection from a man?"

Helen asks, "Is he the type of man that craves attention?"

Jazzman answers, "Very much so and it goes with the territory. I'm on the other side of the business so I see all the dirt and it kills me knowing what can possibly happen if I'm not there with him. Can I get your thoughts on this, but not as a therapist, as if you were a friend."

Helen comments, "Well, if you were a friend and came to me for my opinion I would say, Jazzman, you can't control that. You can only control your behavior. I would also ask you...will you be able to handle his lifestyle in the years to come?"

Jazzman feels a burning sensation inside her chest knowing Helen is right. "I know. I have to find a way to manage my feelings. I feel uneasy before I go, when trying to decide between him and career. You know, when I leave these lavish getaways, reality sinks in and I feel bad about ignoring my work. You would think that I would feel better about the relationship, at least after the getaway, but I don't. It happened again this past weekend when we went away. Not only did I delegate some of my work to a co-worker, I also missed a business opportunity. It's like a piece of me is being chipped away every time I say yes to him and no to my career."

Jazzman has an 'Aha' moment. The two women look at one another and they both feel it. Jazzman experiences a key moment in therapy and realizes this is one of the things that have been eating away at her.

Helen asks, "How does that feel? Answering your own questions."

Jazzman answers, "That felt good. Now, I need to sort out the rest and figure out what's going on with me."

Helen says encouragingly, "You've made great progress today. Let's do this...let's stop here. You have several things going on and before we go any further I want to think about some things you said. Also I want to give you some homework. I want you to start asking yourself if there are things about Afrique that upset you and why?"

Jazzman appears confused and asks, "Why?"

Helen responds, "This will help sort out your feelings since it seems you have the most questions about him in your life right now. I don't mean this to be a negative thing. I just want to help you sort out the feelings you are experiencing and understand how you are internalizing the issue. Then we should start discussing how you would like to move forward. Does that make sense?"

Jazzman smiles, "That makes perfect sense."

Helen adds, "I want you to continue writing in your journal to your mother. If you feel the need to write to your father, do that, too. I think that will help release some of the anger you may hold from feeling abandoned by him. So, continue to write about anything else in your life. And Jazzman, I know the loss of your mother is a huge disconnect. A mother's love is unique and once it's gone nothing can replace it. I want to help you get to a place of understanding that you are not alone. When I say resolve I don't mean completely putting those emotions to rest, but at least coming to terms with it. I want you to feel at peace, to live a fulfilling life without the burden of your past and to have healthy relationships. How does that sound?"

Jazzman answers, "It sounds like exactly what I want."

Helen concludes, "Good! On that note, I have you down on my calendar, for the same time next week. I hope you have a pleasant weekend."

"Thank you. You too." Jazzman leaves the office feeling even better than the first time. She knows it's just the beginning of her sessions, but she feels optimistic about going to therapy. Today she leaves feeling proud that she is taking steps to be in control of her feelings.

MIAMI, FL
Jazzman and Kim

Kim and Jazzman are excited, yet unsure about what to expect at their pole dancing workout. They open the door to an intimate room at the gym they never knew existed, but later discover it was created just for this class. Six poles welcome the group of women who signed up. The sidewalls are mirrored up from floor to ceiling and the corners are decorated with colorful pillows. The dim lights are inviting, bringing a feeling of relaxation and privacy to the room. There is soft R&B playing that somehow helps the women feel relaxed.

A beautiful blue-eyed brunette with full lips and a toned body greets the women with a soft-spoken voice, "Welcome, ladies. My name is, Lindsey, and I'm excited that all of you are here for what will be a rewarding experience. I hope this class becomes a gift to you, a present to your inner being. You will get to know yourself in a personal way and I don't want you to be shy. First, we will go around the room and each of you can tell me your name and why you are here."

The women announce one by one, "My name is, Maggie, and I'm here to feel comfortable in my own skin."

"I'm Pamela and I'm here to learn new tricks to shake things up at the club."

All the women laugh.

The announcements continue, "I'm Jazzman and I'm here because I thought this would be an interesting class. I'm also here to accompany my best friend, Kim."

"I'm Kim, I thought this would be fun and a few months ago my response would have been Pamela's, but since I'm in a relationship now I just want to learn something new. It might even help this developing relationship rise to new heights!" The women clap for Kim.

"My name is Elizabeth. I've been married fifteen years. I'm here to spice up my marriage, not that it needs it, but I'm going to surprise my husband. He's been away for six months in the military, so this will be a nice treat when he returns."

All the women cheer and clap for Elizabeth both on her years of marriage and her quest for excitement.

Lindsey continues her speech, "Again, welcome and I'm glad you took your first step to get to know your body in an intimate way. You may feel awkward at first with the moves in today's session. But, as we get to know each other through these sessions you'll feel more at ease with what you are being asked to do with your body. The best advice I can give you is to relax and let yourself go. Don't feel ashamed. As women, we give so much of ourselves to others, so this class is for you. This is a place where you can unwind and feel sexy…beautiful… at peace. You need to let go in this class. Let go of stress and let go of your troubles that surround you on a daily basis. This is your time, so roll with it and do YOU. Any questions before we get started?"

Elizabeth asks, "Where can we purchase a pole?"

Lindsey answers, "There are two options: a portable one and a permanent one and we can go over that at the end of class. Just remind me. The Vixen Boutique is a great place to go and start looking at some of your options for poles as well as lingerie. You can also pick up some accessories or toys while you are there." Lindsey winks.

Everyone laughs.

Lindsey continues, "Now will be a good time to tell all you ladies that it's okay to wear stilettos in this class. It will help you get into character. First, I'm going to perform a dance on the pole and show you what you will be able to do by the time your six weeks end."

Lindsey walks to the radio, turns the CD to track number three, walks back to the pole and performs to "Sex at the Club" an old R&B song. As Lindsey takes to the pole her body transforms into a butterfly as she twirls around it completely relaxed. She seduces the pole as she slowly slides down and then glides back up with her breasts caressing it. It is a bit daunting to the women who stare in amazement wanting to perform the same routine for their men, but they recognize that athleticism it required. She circles around the pole in a fast, yet inviting way that the women dream of copying. However, they are skeptical as to how they will even learn it all in a few short weeks.

Lindsey then holds her right leg, letting her toes kiss the pole as she touches her fingers to her ankles and slowly, with a hint of seduction, slides them up her leg to her thigh hitting a climax by striking a bad girl pose. All the women grow aroused from her movements. The sensation penetrates through their bodies as they imagine doing the same movements. Afterwards, she lets go of the pole and elegantly drops to the floor for another naughty-girl routine. Just as powerful, touching herself, letting go of her inhibitions, her body screams confidence and enjoyment.

At the end of the dance number all the women clap in amazement, ready to learn their first move.

Before the women get attached to the pole, Lindsey asks the women to describe themselves with one positive word. Several of the women get stuck on this question. Some of them give answers pertaining to work and family. She writes down their responses, but does not explain the reason for the question.

The stretching routine is an exercise to toughen the women's bodies to handle the moves on the pole. They will feel the next day just how out of shape they are, and how in-shape a dancer has to be to work the pole. Everything about the class cries seduction, from the room to the music, down to the moves, its one huge explosion of pleasure and pain.

After the stretch, the women began their session with the basics, slowly circling the pole with passion and a hint of sex appeal. The women are still a bit nervous around each other as well as a bit shy. Not only are they not all that comfortable with their own bodies, they are uneasy showing their intimacy with a group of 'strangers'. Lindsey assures them that each week they will improve and release more of their inhibitions. She also provides them with a tip, "Do whatever moves you, but whenever possible let your assets lead the way. For example, if you are on the ground and need to get up...ASS first. Push it out and let it arouse your man, as you get up in slow motion."

By the end of the class, the shyness was slightly diminishing and they are feeling excited about the next class. They are eager to learn new tricks on the pole.

Pleasure rushes to Jazzman's inner thighs, wishing Afrique were home so she could provoke him with her moves and make love to him in the bedroom.

Kim feels that same rush, but her man, Rick is coming to town. So, her lessons learned will be Rick's gain in the bedroom.

Chapter 6

MIAMI, FL

Jordan, Jackie, Jazzman and Desmond

[Knock! Knock!]

Jazzman waits for someone to answer the door.
Jordan opens it saying, "Hey, Jazz, How are you?"

Jazzman smiles, "I'm good and you?"

"I can't complain. Jackie is trying to find Desmond's baseball glove. Other than that, he is ready." Jordan signals for her to come in.

"Did you see the game last night?" Jordan knows she is referring to the Miami Marlins.

"Yes, amazing last couple of innings…it had me at the edge of my seat."

"Who you telling! A well deserved win. It was an awesome game!" Jazzman pushes down on her baseball cap.

Desmond comes running out of his room yelling, "Jazz!"

She smiles with arms open wide waiting for Desmond to fill her arms with joy. "I missed you. Are you ready for a fun weekend? Daddy can't wait to see you. He should be here tomorrow. He sends his love."

Desmond asks, "Where are we going?"

Jazzman answers, "First, we are going to the park to play some baseball. How does that sound?"

"Cool!"

"Cool!"

Jackie comes down the hall with Desmond's suitcase and she cheerfully calls out, "Hello, Jazzman. It took me a while, but I found his glove."

"How are you, Jackie?"

"I'm well and you?"

"I'm good. Just ready to play some ball." Jazzman looks over at Desmond who has a huge smile on his face.

Jazzman takes the luggage while Jackie and Jordan take turns saying their goodbyes to Desmond.

Jazzman says to Desmond as they walk towards the door, "Say bye, see you on Sunday."

Jackie asks, "Jaz, did Afrique remind you that this is the weekend Jordan and I are going away? He said he would be in town to drop him off and pick him up from school on Monday." Jackie opens the door for them.

Jazzman is puzzled by the news as she is hearing this for the first time. "Oh no, I wasn't aware."

Jackie asks another question, "Is he going to be in town?"

"He must have forgotten to tell me with the tour going on. He's been so busy. If something comes up with his schedule, no worries, I can drop him off and pick him up. I don't think I have any major meetings on Monday. Where are you going?" She asks hoping her frustration does not show. She is upset that Afrique forgot to mention this important detail. Once again, obviously he is not taking her schedule into consideration. Then she stops herself, wondering if she is overreacting.

"To the Keys." Jackie answers with excitement in her voice.

"WELL, you two have fun and don't worry about a thing."

"Okay, be safe, bye!" Jackie and Jordan call out to Desmond as he is getting into the car, "Love you!"

He responds, "Love you, too!"

⌒〇

MIAMI, FL
Jazzman and Desmond

Jazzman and Desmond arrive at the park ready to play some ball. Jazzman adjusts her baseball cap by shaking it from side to side, when it feels right, she yells out to Desmond, "Yuh ready?"

Desmond yells back, "Yes, Jazz."

Desmond and Jazzman start throwing the ball to each other. With each throw they get more competitive, each boasting about their own catch or curve ball, while jokingly making fun of the other.

After playing catch for about an hour, Jazzman allows Desmond to go to the playground with other kids. As she watches him, she moves lightly back and forth on a swing. Suddenly, Jazzman realizes that Afrique has not called to talk to Desmond. She tries to call him, but he does not pick up. She tries one more time and still no answer.

Jazzman calls Desmond over to eat. She had prepared a picnic basket with sandwiches, fruit, chocolate chip cookies and juices for their lunch. After eating they take a relaxing walk around the park.

They head home early in the evening so that Desmond can be ready for bed when his dad calls.

When Jazzman started picking up Desmond while Afrique was traveling, he would always call Desmond to wish him goodnight and let him know he would be home before he wakes up. This night was no different.

However, the next morning, Desmond wakes Jazzman up with disappointment on his face. Although her first reaction was fear, fear that something happened to Afrique, she has to hide it for the sake of Desmond. She hugs him and says playfully, "Let's just call that daddy of yours. Let's find out where he is, and when he's going to get here to put a smile on your face."

"Okay, Jazz." Desmond's worry is beginning to disappear.

She calls Afrique's cell phone. "Good morning. Desmond woke me up wondering where's his daddy. Are you almost here?"

"Jazz, I'm so sorry. I wanted to call you back last night, but it was late. My label sent me to Jamaica for business and TV interviews. I'm so sorry. Can you put Desmond on the phone?"

"Sure." Jazzman hands the phone to Desmond.

Desmond's raspy voice asks, "Daddy, where are you? You said you were going to be here."

"I know little man, but my job sent me to Jamaica and I have to be here for some work stuff. I'm going to make it up to you. I promise."

"Can Jazz and I come see you in Jamaica?"

"I wish you could, but daddy has to work and I won't be able to see you."

"Aw daddy, I want to see you!" Desmond is devastated.

"I know son. I miss you, too, and I will try to make it back on Tuesday. I will ask mommy if I can pick you up from school, so we can go to Wet N Wild. How does that sound?"

"Yaaaay!!!"

'"Good. Now what have you been up to? Are you behaving yourself?"

"Yes, daddy. I'm having fun with Jazzman. She took me to the park."

Afrique smiles, happy to know his son is in good hands when he is not around. "I'm glad you are having a good time. I'll see you soon. Daddy misses you. Let me talk to Jazz."

"Okay, daddy." Desmond hands the phone to Jazzman.

"What's up?"

"Are you okay?" Afrique knows she is upset.

"Just disappointed. We were looking forward to seeing you."

"I know. I'm sorry, but this opportunity is a last minute thing and too good to pass up."

She responds, "Well, thanks for letting me know about Monday."

He's confused, "What's on Monday?"

She continues, "You are supposed to drop Desmond off at school and pick him up."

Afrique is so embarrassed, "Oh man. I'm so sorry, Jazz. I completely forgot. Will you be able to do it for me?"

Jazzman replies with a question, "Yes. See you soon?"

"How about Tuesday? I told Desmond I'll try to pick him up after school if I can set it up with Jackie and maybe we can have a late dinner?" Afrique suggests cheerfully.

Jazzman yawns. "Sounds good. I'll talk to you later. I have to plan something else for Desmond and I to do. I want to make it up to him."

"You are so good to us." Afrique is trying too hard to stay on Jazzman's good side.

"Don't you forget it. Good luck and I will talk to you later, right?" Jazzman asks.

"Yes, I'll call you tonight when I'm finished." Afrique hangs up.

Jazzman hangs up right after and turns to Desmond and says, "Let's pack our bags. You and I are going to drive to Orlando today, so we can go to DISNEY tomorrow!"

Desmond screams in excitement and gives her a big hug. This is not the first time this type of situation has happened, where Jazzman has felt the need to overcompensate just so she could wipe away the sadness on Desmond's face. Jazzman now has a sense of what Jackie has had to endure over the years. She also feels like she is being taken advantage of, as if she is a built in babysitter. This is supposed to be his time with his son and he already spends limited time with him. She's starting to wonder if this is the type of time he will give their son.

There is something else that is bothering her, but she is unable to figure out quite what it is, so she brushes it off assuming that she is probably over-thinking the situation.

As Jazzman sits there for a few minutes she realizes the importance of respecting another woman and the value of a friendship.

She's grateful that she's never tried to steal another woman's man. Her mother taught her from an early age to respect other women and their relationships. She's grateful to have learned this and has formed a sisterhood bond with Kim.

She remembers one time in her life where she hated having female bosses. Then Gina had come along - a well-groomed, confident woman who led Jazzman on the right path. The sometimes challenging boss-to-employee relationship had developed into mutual respect and then eventually a great friendship. Jazzman found she was able to learn so much from Gina and still keep their friendship separate from their business roles.

Jazzman remembers what Gina had gone through, and the pain of dealing with her cheating husband. She's glad she was able to be there for Gina and from that experience she learned why a woman should not mess with another woman's marriage. She's happy to have her dignity and her self-respect. It's what she needs right now, some strength to pull through for Desmond, as she begins to pack their things for Orlando, FL. She does not want to be angry so she recites the prayer to herself, "GOD grant me the serenity to accept the things I can not change, COURAGE to change the things I can, and WISDOM to know the difference. Amen."

MIAMI, FL
Tyson and His Parents

Tyson opens the door, shouting, "Momma, I'm home." When there is not a response he goes to the backyard and sure enough his mom is outside with his dad. His dad is at the grill and his mom is on the hammock reading a book.

Tyson goes up to his pops first since he is closer, gives him a manly hug, then greets her with a kiss and reinforces it with a hug.

"So what are you two love birds up to?"

Mr. and Mrs. Banks look at one another smiling. They look at their son and almost in unison saying, "What do you want?"

Tyson smiles as well. "Oh, it's like that? That's how you greet your son? It's not what I want, it's what I have to tell you."

His mother gives him a look that says 'don't lie because I can see right through you', "Boy, you better not be making me a grand-mother already and out of wedlock?"

Tyson still smiling, "Come on, the only way that scenario will play out is with Jazzman, and you know her situation, so you know you can put that to rest."

Mr. Banks adds his opinion. "Boy, you have to be more like your dad. You see how I got your mother to come to her senses and real-ize she needed to be with me."

They all start laughing, and Mrs. Banks breaks the laughter by asking, "What's going on baby? What do you need to tell us?"

"My job is promoting me!"

Mr. and Mrs. Banks respond simultaneously to congratulate their son.

He puts up his hands, pumping the brakes on their joy when he adds, "It's in New York. Same company, but the job is in New York. It's not permanent, but I will be there six months to a year."

"Baby, that's too long! Will you be making trips back here?" Mrs. Banks asks not wanting her baby boy to leave for what seems to her like a long time. As an only child, Tyson's mom tends to baby him and he is okay with it.

"Nope, I will be there for the length of time they need me. Of course I can come back for a long weekend. But I might stay there, depending on how things go. However I don't want to look too far into the future. One day at a time and I'll see how things pan out, because I need the change of scenery. I've been here since I was a toddler, so I might use my vacation time to travel up north. The two of you are welcome to visit me. Visit your roots, what do you say?"

Mr. Banks flips the steaks, "I think we can arrange time. We can visit family. It will be nice to go back north for a visit, but only in the summer. Our bones can't take the cold winters anymore."

Mrs. Banks reflects back on the years in New York City. Knowing it's the perfect place for her son and his career, she asks, "So when does this change take effect?"

"In another month or so. My boss and his assistant are still finalizing all the details."

"We will need to plan a special cook-out before you leave…invite friends and family." Mrs. Banks adds with sentiment in her voice.

"That sounds like a plan, Ma…always lookin' out for your son."

Mr. Banks asks, "What about me? Who's gonna look out for me?"

Tyson pats his dad on the back and says, "Don't worry pops, Ma has enough love for both of us. Besides, I always got your back."

Mr. Banks says, "By the way son, are you ready for your vacation to New Orleans? Also, I did some investigating for you. Once I have more details lets sit down and discuss a game plan."

Tyson pats his dad on the back again, "Thanks, Pops. I appreciate it."

Mrs. Banks adds, "That's right, how long are you staying?"

"Actually, plans have changed there, too. It will also be a business trip. Jazzman put together a proposal for us to go, so my vacation will be expensed. It should be nice."

Mrs. Banks blushes, "So you two are going away together before you go to New York?"

Mr. Banks takes the steaks and corn on the cob off the grill, completely oblivious to his wife's subliminal message. "You will have a nice time with Jazzman."

Mrs. Banks and Tyson look at each other and smile thinking the same thing. How did Mr. Banks, a retired detective, miss that one? Tyson was speechless; he smiles and shakes his head.

Mr. Banks prepares the plates and sits down next to his wife. She thanks him and they both gaze at one another for a few seconds.

Tyson smiles at their admiration for one another. "What's going on with you two? What telepathic message are you two sending to one another again? Please share." He loved watching the interaction between his mother and father. The couple has been together so long and their chemistry is still vibrant and in some ways stronger than when they first united as a couple. They had their share of conflict and arguments, but their love for one another was far stronger than any difference of opinion.

Mrs. Banks answers, "Oh nothing, baby, we are just happy for you. But we will be sad to see you go. We know it's to further your career, so we are mostly happy for you."

Mr. Banks blesses the meal, and they dig in. Grilled steaks and corn on the cob was an all time favorite at the Banks household. It was the perfect way to celebrate their son's promotion.

MIAMI, FL
Jazzman

On Monday morning, Jazzman drops Desmond off at school and goes to work tired from her activity-filled weekend with him. The bond between them is growing and giving her a better understanding of motherhood. However, her longing to have children soon is now postponed, because she realizes motherhood is no joke. She now understands the message, 'it's not as easy as one thinks.' She used to look at people raising their kids and question their way of parenting. Now, she only holds respect for those who are doing the best they can.

Through her relationship with Afrique she is being exposed to the difference between a woman's role and a man's role in a child's life. Although she recognizes some of the reasons for the differences in the gender roles, she understands the need for it to be dual responsibility.

In her culture, it is definitely the women who play the more significant role in the child's life, but her upbringing in America makes her question that theory. She's had her dad abandon her. She sees how Afrique puts work before his son; she wonders if it wasn't for Afrique's job would he be there for his son? She is glad she had this experience with Desmond because it's making her question things and she will bring it up in her therapy session on Thursday.

By Thursday, Jazzman is ready to get through her workday. She is looking forward to her afternoon therapy session to release her feelings. The gloomy day filled with dark clouds makes the time go by slowly and only adds fuel to the fire because her thoughts are consuming her. From time to time she jots things down to bring up at therapy.

When Jazzman arrives at Helen's office she is all fired up to get things off her chest. Helen is ready for it, knowing from years of experience that by the third or fourth visit patients are often discovering and viewing their problems in a new light. However she also knows this step only happens when one is not resisting therapy. She recognizes that Jazzman is willing to explore some of the feelings buried inside her.

What set Jazzman off this week is Afrique's failure to make it home for Desmond's weekend visit. This has happened before, but this time it somehow struck Jazzman differently. It bothered her more than ever before and it's setting off a red flag that Jazzman is unable to explain. But before she goes into this past weekend, she discusses the results of her homework from last week. She opens up, by listing them one by one from the first day they met.

She goes into detail about the several times Afrique tried to be with her, but still not cutting the relationship ties with Jackie as he said he would. It's those moments with Afrique, where he is not honest with her that is causing her a great deal of pain. She explains to Helen that her whole relationship with Afrique has been an emotional rollercoaster from the moment they met. It's also causing her to question their love. She's unsure if it's worth the battle.

She also tells Helen about her planned revenge on Afrique for seeing him with Jackie that last night in Jamaica. She tells her about the next day when she gives Afrique a taste of his own medicine by showing up at one of his events with Tyson. She confesses that she purposely planted doubt in his mind about her friendship with Tyson. She admits that she is the reason for causing friction between the two men.

Jazzman also opens up about Tyson's feelings towards her, her feelings towards him and their relationship from college up to this point in their lives. She explains the importance of Tyson in her life and how he's been that positive stability that she needs.

After she is done, she brings up this past weekend with Afrique. She questions the role he will play as a husband and father. It does not match up with the type of family she envisioned for her own. She doesn't know if it is fair to question these things knowing he is a good man. At the same time she has to take into account their life-styles and their hang-ups due to the lives they live. She questions if it will balance out or cause conflict. She feels that a relationship should have shared responsibility of regular life duties.

As she explains her life, she begins to realize just how many chances she has given Afrique without confronting him about her feelings towards his actions. She questions if she is running away from her problems by not talking about it with him.

Helen helps her examine her feelings. She also questions her and helps her realize the connection between her relationship with her father and her relationship with Afrique. Afrique and her dad are both musicians and they both have had a hard time staying monoga-mous. The similarities makes Jazzman wonder if she is with him in part to get that missing piece of her life.

Helen's questions help Jazzman realize how many unresolved issues she is holding on to. And maybe, just maybe, there were other reasons for needing Tyson in her life. Is he more than just a best friend? She discovers just how bad she needs answers and some of those answers relate to her relationship with her dad. Maybe the resolution means she needs to finally search for him. She wonders deep down inside if the reason she has not been able to put her mother's passing to rest is due to the missing link, her dad. She knows it has been a barrier that has held so many uncertainties, and wonders if it's the key to feel at peace.

After the session, as Jazzman drives home in the rain, she feels more at ease. She is grateful that she is beginning to understand more about who she is, and although it has been a struggle, she is enjoying the journey of discovery.

She arrives home, with time to spare before meeting up with Kim for their class. She puts her things down and just takes a moment to rest on the sofa and breathe. Although she is learning a lot about herself, it's mentally draining. Her head has been pounding with thoughts. She tries to minimize the power of those thoughts by rationalizing it. *My problems are small in comparison to the things that are going on in this world. Yes, I have a right to be mad. My dad wasn't there, but I can't continue to live in the past. I can't continue to blame him for all my problems. I have to grow up at some point and let my past be my past. I have control of right now. So I can't continue to sit around and feel sorry for myself. Life is too damn short. There are so many things that go on in the world from wars to earthquakes...loved ones unexpectedly pass in horrible ways... those people hurt and somehow find strength to carry on. I must do the same. Yet, I can't help but wonder if I'm wrong for feeling the way I do about Afrique. He is working hard, doing his thing and taking me to beautiful places with him. I also have a wonderful step-son that I adore. These two men are my family now and I should appreciate my life. I feel so wrong for going to therapy and bashing him. I have a wonderful life despite the crap I've been through. All relationships are not perfect. I know there will be times I will not be able to meet up with Afrique when he asks me. I'm going to have to be strong and be honest with him. He might not like it, but hopefully he will understand and still find a way to stay committed to me and ease my worries.*

She takes five additional minutes to meditate before meeting up with Kim. This time she is looking forward to having fun at class and releasing the heavy stuff taking up space in her mind.

∽⊙

MIAMI, FL
Jazzman and Kim

[Music - Soft Melody Playing]

As the women walked into their second pole dancing class they were greeted with a glass of wine and assorted appetizers. The burning candles gave off soothing spa aromas. The scent alone is enough to leave the stress at the door. A complimentary hand massage is an unexpected pleasure. This is Lindsey's way of demonstrating to the women just how easy it is to set the mood and spice up an evening for two.

Once the ladies have some wine in their system, they venture into the art of stripteasing. Their first lesson is to walk the walk. Each woman is instructed to strut her stuff. Lindsey walks them through the motion of swaying their hips like a figure eight, placing one foot in front of the other and parading around the room. She reminds them that their partner loves confidence, so she calls out, "Chest out, head up! Be proud of what God gave you. Think sassy! It's all about attitude, ladies. If you are uncomfortable imagine that you are leading your partner into the bedroom."

She informs them that stripping is like unwrapping a special gift. She says, "You have to approach it like you are slowly peeling off one layer at a time. You want to keep your partner guessing at what will happen next…will you remove a piece of clothing? Are you going to give in? Or are you going to give him a performance he will never forget? A lap dance? My answer is 'No'! I know it's tempting, but ladies, you want to resist giving in. You even want to resist touching until you are done with your entire performance. Instead, you are going to touch and caress your body making him/her hungry until they can't take it anymore and they are tempted to touch. Keep your eyes on the prize. In other words, maintain eye contact and make his or her ass wait…however you like it served to you."

Lindsey's last statement causes laughter to fill the room.

Lindsey continues as the women begin to remove one piece of their clothing very slowly, "Remember, you are SEXY. You will feel it when you have that naughty lacy lingerie underneath your clothing. So *mamacitas,* believe it! You don't have to be a supermodel. You are perfect just the way you are…so touch yourself slowly and draw attention to your favorite body parts. If you have trouble with this, imagine…imagine his hands on your body. Close your eyes for a few seconds as you touch and when you feel the sensation, look at him so he can crave your body."

As Kim is absorbing this information, she begins to imagine putting this to use the next time Rick is in town. She can't wait to put him into a trance. Kim is taking mental notes as Lindsey is showing them how to use a scarf as a playful thing or as an item to tie their partner's hands.

Jazzman feels like she is always rushing to take off clothes when she is in the mood so she is learning how to slowly take it off, one item at a time. She likes the delay tactics, and it will really turn her on to watch Afrique's excitement. She too can't wait to use these lessons and let it play out in the bedroom. She learns what items not to wear, and techniques on removing difficult clothing, as well as how to pace the performance.

The women love the power of a stance and are having fun practicing it. They all form a circle with their backside facing the center pretending their partner is in the middle. They all look over their shoulder and strike a pose to their imaginary partner. After a few practice shots the women begin to strike various poses until it becomes amusing.

Then they are instructed to seductively turn around to face their imaginary partner and make eye contact. They are encouraged to take it one step further, placing their right hand above their heart and elegantly stroking it down their center, turning the hand to stroke the waistline, all the way down their thigh. For some, this is out of their comfort zone and to perform it around other women feels awkward.

Before class ends, Lindsey puts on another spectacular show for the women. They watch as their instructor puts into action the moves she has taught them in class. Each seductive pose provokes the viewer wanting to feel what their eyes are witnessing. Watching Lindsey helps them see the full picture, as if it were a piece of artwork coming to life. It was an encouraging way to end the class, it gave the women a boost of confidence.

Chapter 7

MIAMI, FL
Jazzman, Kim, Rick and Tyson

Kim is on her way to pick up Rick at the airport. He will only be in town for two days, so Kim has to make good use of the time they have together. They go straight to South Beach to meet up with Tyson and Jazzman for drinks.

From the moment Rick and Tyson meet, the two hit it off. The four of them are sitting at a table near the bar, drinking and talking over the loud music. As they talk, they watch the people on the dance floor jammin' to the music.

As the night goes on, Tyson and Rick find that they can share their appreciation for beautiful women. From time to time, they tap each other underneath the table to point out a hottie walking by or shaking her ass near their table. Those 'boy' moments with Rick, gets Tyson fired up knowing he will have a cool cat to hang out with in New York, not a stiff brother unable to admire beautiful women just because he's 'in love.' It's no secret that Tyson loves women. He loves the chase and he loves a new challenge. Therefore, when a woman tells him no, he works his charm to get past that "no" and boost his male ego, letting it be known to himself that, "I still got it!"

After several hours at the bar, Jazzman calls it an early night, knowing tomorrow she is about to do the unthinkable. Tyson leaves shortly after to give the two lovebirds their time alone.

Kim and Rick take advantage of the time by walking in the moonlight on South Beach. It's a perfect evening to enjoy the fresh air, the pleasant aromas that Rick is not accustomed to, living in New York.

Very little talking is done, as they soak in the ambiance from the music to the people laughing, having a good time. They listen to the waves as they make their way to shore leaving an imprint on the sand. They hold one another sharing a special moment, to make up for the times they will be far apart.

MIAMI, FL
Rick, Kim and Kim's Mom

When Kim and Rick wake up in the morning, they rent a motorcycle and hop on Route 95 towards Tampa to meet Kim's mom, Patsy.

When they ring the doorbell, Patsy rushes to greet Kim and Rick. The smell of southern home-style cooking welcomes them: macaroni and cheese, fried chicken, collard greens, barbeque ribs and corn bread. In the past Kim and her mom could barely be in the same room together, Patsy has mended her old ways and apologized to Kim for her behavior. Living hours apart helps them have a less contentious relationship. Kim's decision to bring a guy to meet her mom is a big deal and Patsy is hoping that this is a sign of a fresh start to their relationship. It's something Patsy has prayed for a healed relationship with her daughter. She greatly regrets the pain she has caused Kim through the choices she made with men as a young mother.

Kim hugs her. "Hi, mom. Mom, this is Rick. Rick, this is my mom, Patricia Mills, but everyone calls her Patsy."

Rick reaches out to shake her hand, "Hello, Ms. Mills, it's a pleasure to meet you."

"Likewise, but you can call me Patsy. Make yourselves at home. I need to finish setting the table." Patsy is very pleased that Rick looks like a nice guy, not like some of the thugs her daughter used to bring home years ago. Back then, when Patsy attempted to discuss her choices with men, a huge argument ensued and Kim stopped bringing guys around. Kim did not want her mother providing advice on a topic that she had no business preaching on. At least that is how Kim viewed it after all those painful years growing up. Her mom knows there is still a lot of tension between them and she knows that it will take a really good heart-to-heart conversation to begin putting the past behind them. However, Patsy feels that Kim is still not ready to fight those demons.

Rick seems to sense an undercurrent of tension between the two women and wonders about its cause. Having known what it's like to live without a mother, Rick does not want Kim to take her relationship for granted.

When Patsy excuses herself, Kim turns to Rick and says, "Why don't you sit and see what's on TV. I'm going to help my mom."

Rick smiles and says, "I think you should relax, kick your lovely feet up on this sofa, and watch TV or you can close your eyes for a few minutes. I will help your 'momz' in the kitchen. This way she can ask me all the questions she wants and I can slide in a few about you. How does that sound?"

Kim blushes and chuckles. "I actually like that idea."

Rick winks at her, "Okay."

Kim is happy. For the first time she is not feeling ashamed of who she is and although bringing Rick to meet her mother feels a little awkward, she knows he is different. She feels it and hopes her intuition is on point. Her mother will be getting to know a new Kim, one that is growing and changing for the better. She hopes that it can bring them closer and her mom will stop giving her 'personal opinion' on her choices going forward.

Meanwhile, in the kitchen Rick surprises Patsy when he asks, "Okay, Ms. Mills, I mean Patsy, how can I be of assistance to you?"

Patsy smiles. "Well, let's see. You can mix the collard greens. The big spoon is on the left side of the stove."

As Rick goes about his duty, Patsy asks, "So, Rick, are you enjoying your stay in Miami?"

"Yes, ma'am, and I'm spending time with an awesome lady."

Patsy smiles at his response. "That she is! She said you are from New York, correct?"

Rick responds, "Yes, I live in Brooklyn."

Patsy inquires as bluntly as possible, "How do you feel about a long distance relationship with my daughter, you being a man and all? You and I know a man has needs and if they are not being met, he's going to shop around for the next pretty little thing. You see where I'm going with this?"

Rick is unsure how to handle her bold statement, but in a way it reminds him of his mother, so he hints with a smile, "I hear you, Patsy, but I'm at a different point in my life. I like your daughter a lot and I want to explore the feelings she and I share. Some married couples are around each other their whole lives and are miserable. So I don't want to condemn the relationship just because of distance when the feelings we share are real. We have both decided to take it one day at a time. We don't know where the road ahead will lead us, but for now we are just two souls living in the moment."

Rick is unable to see the tears that have surfaced on Patsy's face. She finds it odd that one statement from Rick could bring her to that state, but it's likely because he sounds genuine. He is not making big promises, and he is being honest. She wonders if this is a sign, a hint of hope, that one of her prayers is finally being answered. "I hear you. I just don't want you misleading my daughter, you hear. I've already put that girl through enough and she needs a good man holding her down. I know you two are just getting to know each other and it's too soon to be stating this, but for future reference I have to state it. If you ever want out just be upfront with her. She deserves that much from you, being that she is taking a chance with you far away from her. I just want to put that out there if this relationship begins to blossom."

"I hear you. So, can I ask you a question?"

"Shoot." Patsy answers as she hands the plates of corn bread and macaroni and cheese to Rick to place on the table.

"What was Kim like growing up?"

Patsy ponders what to say, "Uh...Kim was a bit rough around the edges, and so many of her choices in life were brought on by my selfishness and my choices in life. I didn't do as good a job as I could have raising her. But, when she is ready she will talk to you about her upbringing." She places her hand on Rick's arm and stresses, "When she is ready, okay?"

Rick's expression shifts to a look of concern. After a moment, he answers confidently, "I promise, Patsy."

"Thank you." She pats him on the arm.

After placing the dishes on the table, Rick calls Kim to the kitchen. The food smells good. Patsy places big heaps of food on their plates. Rick is grateful for the barbeque ribs and after a few bites he prays that Kim knows how to make them just like her mom. The fried chicken is, and always will be, Kim's favorite.

They take their time eating all the delicious food. Afterwards, they sit out on the front porch for light conversation. They talk about Kim growing up and how she was such a stubborn little girl with an attitude, though always full of life. Rick enjoys learning about Kim and knowing he may have his hands full. He is okay with it, because he genuinely is enjoying his time with her.

Rick and Kim cut their time short with Patsy so they can spend more time alone. Patsy would love more time getting to know Rick, but she doesn't want to stress Kim. However, given the conversation she had with him earlier, it appears that Rick has good intentions, and she is okay with what she has learned of him, so far. Her main concern is the distance between them. Her prayers will have to suffice in that matter. She takes a moment to pray that if things don't work out, he will still serve as a stepping-stone in the right direction for her daughter.

MIAMI, FL
Kim and Rick

Rick and Kim venture off on their ride back down the Florida coast to her apartment in Miami. They decide to spend the evening at home with rented movies and popcorn. Before pressing play on the DVD, some romance is set in motion, a movie of their own as Kim gravitates towards the pole to indulge her man. She knows it will serve as a perfect treat.

Before getting into character, she asks, "Do you trust me?"

He is confused as to why she is asking, but he answers, "So far, yes."

"Will you trust me to wrap this around your hands, so I can strip-tease for you?" She asks with a sad puppy look on her face as she holds a black silk scarf in her hand.

"Now, I understand. Yes I will and yes, you may."

"Okay. Wait here. I need to get ready for my debut with you as my audience. Don't move. I will be right back." Kim is so excited, she rushes into her room to take her clothes off, slips on her lingerie and puts her clothes over it to surprise him even more. She runs back out and says, "I'm back...did you miss me?"

"Yes...but, I thought you were going to change or something like that?"

As she sits on top of him with her inner thighs touching his man-hood she begins to tie his wrists together behind his back as she answers, "I did, but you'll just have to wait for the show to begin. Then you'll understand the storyline."

"Okay, I'm the director and I call action."

Kim wants to stay straddling him. Rick feels good and letting him slip into her right now would be pleasurable, but she stands up. Kim has to use all her will power to walk away and press play on the CD player, because what she is about to perform will be worth the wait.

As the music begins, so does her body, swaying to the music. Her fingertips move slowly up her thighs, stopping at the waistline teasing with a hint of what is underneath her shirt. She continues the journey past her breast and up to her neck as she strikes a seductive pose for her man. Her curious fingers find their way back down to her breasts, touching them as her gaze connects with Rick and his hazel eyes widen in excitement. He wants to jump her bones, but he knows more is in store if he holds out and lets Kim entertain him. She definitely knows how to set him off.

She brings her hands back down over her skin tight jeans to her inner thighs to spread her legs, opening them slowly letting her hips rock from side to side. The way she is moving her body is making Rick go insane. She repositions herself to provide Rick with a side profile of her lady lump. She rotates it in small circular motion letting him see and imagine how good it will feel once she is making love to him.

She works her backside and waistline to the beat of the music all the way down to the floor. As she learned in class, she continues her quest by obsessively 'cat-walking' her way to Rick who waits in anticipation. Her tongue takes a seductive voyage on Rick's neck, followed by her juicy lips sealing it with a dose of passion.

She slowly pulls away rocking her body into a full profile. Inch by inch she begins to take off her shirt to reveal part of her lingerie. To expose the bottom half she unbuttons her jeans, pausing, swaying her body from side to side to the beat of the music. As she unzips, she simultaneously gives him a backside view sticking her buttocks out to entice his eyes as the pants roll down her legs little by little, exposing her naked skin and the v-string riding her full moon. It has Rick reaching out for Kim as he undoes the knot on the scarf that is preventing him from touching what is now his. As he leans his body in towards hers, her physique pushes back into his as he sways, their midsections melting into one another.

However, Kim still has more in store. She gently pushes him back down on the sofa, making his blood pressure rise as she teases him some more by gravitating towards the pole and stroking it erotically down to the ground and back up. She lusciously twirls around the pole, landing her pose to face Rick, winking at him. She works her body into a floor routine extending her long legs out to the air, taking her fingers to caress and stroke her skin passing her knees up to her waist, calling him over to join her. He is mesmerized by her sex appeal and their bodies reunite on the floor. This time he ties her wrists together so his tongue can seduce every inch of her body, tasting her sweat, her passion and smelling the scent of her perfume.

He gazes deeply into her eyes and asks, "I don't know if I'm going to be able to leave tomorrow. How do I say 'bye', when all I wanna do is stay?"

Kim smiles nervously. "I feel the same way when I visit you. It's hard to leave the man I want. That's why I did all this for you. I'm scared of us failing at this when I really need you in my life. You feel right and I don't want us to lose the momentum between us due to distance. Know what I mean?"

Rick responds, "I hear you. You do know you don't have to do all this to keep me interested in you, right? Although, a brother is not complaining! You can do this anytime. As long as we are honest with one another, even when we are feeling vulnerable, I think we will be okay. We can talk each other out of doing something we will regret. I like what we have, so give your man a kiss."

Kim does just that, pressing her lips against his. "We also have the best damn phone sex."

"Yes, we do!" As Rick says this, Kim gets up and moves quickly toward the bedroom getting a head start and says, "Last one to the room has to cook breakfast."

Kim of course beats him.

"Oh, it's like that?" He chases after her, pinning her down on the bed.

She responds whispering, "Yes, it's like that and I want the works tomorrow morning."

"What about right now? What do you want right now?" Before she could respond, Rick embraces her, showering her with his lips. Each kiss penetrates through her body, his touch brings her to feel a level of emotion she never gave herself permission to feel in her previous relationships.

Kim pulls her shirt off answering his question, "Right now, I want you."

⌒◡

BOCA RATON, FL
Kim and Rick

A romantic date awaits Rick and Kim as they set foot into Boca Raton's, Love Seat Movies, an Asian-themed palace theater, which caters to couples. Kim had heard that the restaurant at the theater has great food. It's recommended to have a meal before the movie, because after the movie, sweet bites of love behind closed doors is the best dessert. It's a recipe for an awesome way to end the evening.

When they enter the theater featuring, "Power Is Mine", they were blown away by the decor. The theater's Asian patterned seats were red and black with gold trimming. The accents on the wall were Asian calligraphy and the dark cherry polished bentwood flowing along the walls and ceilings gave it a rich feel. It is inviting and relaxing, a perfect place for couples.

They rest their cocktails on the side table. Smiling Kim says, "I'm so glad you are here with me."

Rick wraps his arm around her, "I don't want to go back. I love being in Miami with you. I feel so relaxed when I'm in town. The city life brings on such a tough guy attitude and when I get here I just feel so at ease."

Kim is touched by his comment, "Really?"

"Yes! It's a whole different atmosphere. I really love it here—"

Rick grows silent when the movie begins. As they watch the film it brings back painful memories for both Kim and Rick. However, what they will find out later is how the movie brings them closer.

The movie brings on dark memories, so they agree to go for a stroll to de-stress. Rick laces his hand with hers as they walk a few blocks down from the theater to Mizner Park. Holding her hand is his safety net to get the courage for what he is about to share with her. First, Rick decides to reiterate what she stated when they exited the movie theater, "That movie was crazy. What did you like about it?"

For Kim the film brought out so much of her childhood that it's hard to answer the question. "Well...I will have to say...actually...I really like the way Ashley played both men to get what she wanted for her career. So many times you see smart women getting played by men. The men are either bringing drama into the relationship or cheating on women. It was nice to see it played the other way around."

Rick smiles, "I thought you would like that part. But you know... some girls let themselves get played by guys. They keep taking the guy back when he cheats, lies or mistreats. Women should trust their intuition to know something is not right, value themselves more and let the dude go when things go sour."

Kim sees his point. "Agreed, but that also sounds like trust issues. I think sometimes people are looking for the perfect person with no flaws and that is not possible. I'm starting to learn that people need to work on themselves before they can find someone that is compatible. You need to be okay with who you are before you can be okay with someone else in your life."

"Agreed. To be honest, that movie was similar to my life story. I can relate to certain parts of the movie." Rick says as he gestures for them to sit at a park bench overlooking the water fountain with cultivated plant life surrounding it. The scenery is soothing to the eye and brought calmness to the spirit. They take a moment to admire the view.

Kim sits down and Rick sits facing her. Kim thought she sensed which scenes in the movie was a reflection of his life, but she asks any way. "They story line hit home for me as well. Which parts did you relate to?"

"The stuff about Killa's mom spoke to me. It bothered me because at least she raised her son...I mean...I know it's a movie and all, but that hurt me. Remember how I told you my mom was addicted to drugs? Kim, I was given up for adoption. The man who raised me, who I consider my dad, also raised two other adopted boys. I'm grateful for my dad. He did an amazing job raising us, but it hurts having an absent mother. Well, back to my mom...remember how I told you that I've looked for her? Well, she is still strung on drugs. I've had no luck in finding her, but she knows where I live. I'm hoping that one day she will come back a clean woman and that is why I don't want to leave New York. I'm holding onto faith that one day she will recover and come see me."

Kim feels a deep compassion for Rick's struggle. Although she has not suffered through his issues, she understands the hurt and can relate given her own relationship issues with her mom. "Wow, that has got to be a hard thing to go through. Mothers are supposed to be the ones that nurture their children, make them feel safe and secure. I'm so sorry for your pain. Did you go to various foster homes? How old were you when you were taken from your mom?"

Rick begins to feel sad as he relives the memories. "I was about six years old. Prior to that, I remember my grandmother taking care of me almost every day. When she passed away, I became a ward of the state since my mother was in no condition to raise me. I moved from home to home, but I connected with the social worker that was assigned to my case. To make a long story short, he eventually became my dad. He was passionate about his work. He was well off, and could afford to raise us. He was married before he adopted us, but his wife died of cancer. She was not able to have children and wanted to adopt. So he fulfilled her wishes. Once he had me he could not stop there. He wanted me to have siblings. So, when he felt that same connection he adopted two other boys. He only wanted boys because his philosophy is a man knows how to raise a boy and help him become a man."

Kim stops him to make sure she has it right, "So, there's your dad, two brothers and you, right?"

"Yes. We had our share of rough times due to what we were born into, but we overcame that due to the love we had from our father. Although it's a good life, I still miss my mom. I still want to save her. I went through an emotional rollercoaster trying to get through to her, but it's useless. I finally had to let it go."

"Wow, Rick, I would have never guessed that you have been through all this stuff growing up. Your demeanor, your character gives me the impression that you come from a stable home with a white picket fence. I thought two parents raised you, and they taught you the fundamentals of life. Know what I mean?"

Rick smiles. "Thank you. Well, I guess you can thank my dad because he did give my brothers and I that foundation. He raised us to treat others the way we want to be treated. He's a wise man. We let him know all the time that his Father's Day is every day because he saved us."

Hearing how proud he is of his dad brought Kim's tears to surface once again. "Your dad gave you and your brothers guidance and feelings of security. I wish I had had that growing up."

Rick looks puzzled knowing there is more to Kim's story, but not sure she is ready to share. "I don't understand, I thought your mom raised you?"

"She did, technically speaking, but it's the way I was raised. What I witnessed and what I had to endure led to endless therapy sessions that never did much good. That was partly my fault, because I wasn't ready to open up and relive everything I went through." She looks at Rick to gauge his reaction, to see if he's ready to leave her. In her old neighborhood, guys hearing a woman has been to therapy would be viewed as a red flag.

"So what are some of the things you went through?" Rick gazes into her eyes to signal it's okay to open up and he holds her hand to make it known that he is not going anywhere.

"Where do I begin?" Kim feels the tears stinging. "My mom was not there for me as a child. Men were the only ones she entertained. I hated seeing numerous men in and out of our apartment - most walking in just for sex, some staying for a while with her, but each relationship would end up in either verbal or physical abuse." Kim tears up, "Those relationships became the norm to me. Up until six months ago, I was following the same pattern. I allowed men to mistreat me, too. I was addicted to having drama in my life. I kept searching for love in everyone else instead of loving myself. I'm still trying to get there. Every day is a struggle for me mostly because I have so much anger. I'm mad at the way things went down. I'm angered that my mother was selfish and did not raise me to be a lady. She should have taught me to respect myself and not put a man's needs before mine." Kim tries to wipe away some of the tears, but as she wipes, even more emerge.

Rick reaches for a napkin in his pocket and wipes her tears as he whispers, "Are you okay? Do you want to continue this some other time? Is it too much?"

Kim allows her gaze to connect with his, for once feeling safe with someone else. Unfamiliar emotions take over, as she says to herself what she can't say out loud to Rick, *I think I love you.* A lump forms in her throat because she feels at peace with him. "I'm okay. This actually feels good. I've had this bottled up for so long and for the first time I want to let it out. I want to share my story with you."

"Thank you, I'm honored. You know your past is safe with me. I'm not going to judge you. I've seen a lot and I've been through quite a bit myself, so I'm here for you as long as you'll have me."

Kim wants to know if he is for real, "Don't make promises until you've heard my story, there is more."

"Kim, I know with time you will open up to me. I want to be here for you and make you feel safe in my arms." Rick gently places his hands on her cheeks and looks into her eyes. The look feeds love into her soul as he says it again, "I'm here for you and I'm not going anywhere." Before either of them can begin to assess the emotions that have infiltrated and embodied their spirits, he adds, "I love you."

Almost immediately and without pause, Kim's soft voice echoes, "I love you, too."

Rick leans in and seals his lips with hers, slowly allowing his tongue to capture hers. She feels his love seeping through her pores, permitting the beautiful sensation to flow through her body, chipping away the barrier of anger. The anger she has built up over the years. She begins to feel his love as it replace the negative feelings with trust. Without even realizing it, she feels the slightest hint of betrayal to her race. Then seconds later she comes to her senses realizing love has no color, love has no boundaries, love is allowing yourself to connect with another person, allowing that person to get to know the real you and being okay with your imperfections. His sensitivity allows her to open up, giving her soul the reassurance she needs to take a chance and feel real love.

Chapter 8

NEW YORK CITY, NY

Jazzman

Jazzman for the first time finds herself being reactive instead of proactive. She is about to make a move that is not compatible with her values. It's a move that she feels only desperate people do when they need answers. If a friend were in her position, she would say, 'If you have to go to that length, you are not in the best situation and should let him go.' However, she finds herself flying to New York to 'surprise' Afrique, but this isn't an exciting surprise visit to her man. It's a decision based on her gut. She has been wondering what her man is up to. It's a decision she made based on her female intuition.

Her timing will be impeccable, if she arrives right before his opening act gets on stage. It will give them some time alone to catch up after him being missing in action the past weekend. Jazzman's heart is racing as she pulls up to the coliseum. When she arrives, she feels a little strange walking down the long tunnel to get backstage. As she turns the corner and gets closer to the crowd of people backstage, she witnesses Diamond, a singer from New York, smiling and flirting with her man, invading his personal space.

Before Jazzman could continue her eavesdropping, someone from Afrique's camp shouts, "What up, Jazz?"

She is pissed, wondering if they were alerting Afrique. She responds, "Hello!"

The emcee is heard backstage as he draws the crowd's attention, "Let me introduce to you a woman with a flawless, sexy body and smooth, caramel skin. Ladies, you better watch out...hold on tight to your man. Fellaz, I got a glimpse backstage and she is HOT! She has that sex appeal and her touch can leave a man intoxicated for 'dayz'. Fellaz, do you understand what I'm saying? Am I making any sense right now? Cause just the thought of her has my mind twisted, so allow me to introduce to you a rare, exquisite gem, DIAMOND!"

The crowd cheers for Diamond as she works the stage from the moment she steps on. Jazzman can't help but feel nauseous as the crowd cheers for her. A hint of jealousy is what she is sensing, but she won't admit it. Jazzman hates that she is on tour with Afrique. Diamond always rubbed her the wrong way. It's the reason why she did not sign her to Irie Land Records a few years ago. Now she wonders if that was the right thing to do, since she is blowing up the charts and on tour with Afrique, a chart-topping artist. She always sensed that Diamond had potential, but felt her attitude would hold her back. Did she misjudge Diamond?

She tries to block off what is happening on stage to focus her attention on Afrique, who is surprised to see her. "What's up? Are you okay? Is Desmond okay?"

Jazzman answers, "We're good. I thought I'd surprise you to see how you're doing. I want to make sure you are okay. Is your label overworking you?"

"Yah, you know how it is. I'm sorry I couldn't make it. How did Desmond take it?"

"Like I told you before, he was heart-broken. I think I cheered him up by taking him to Disney. We had a good time." Jazzman smiles thinking of Desmond and the good time they had going from ride to ride, sometimes lining back up again and again for his favorite rides.

"What are you smiling about?" Afrique asks reciprocating the smile.

"Just thinking of Desmond. You have an amazing son. I enjoy spending time with him."

"Really, so when are we going to have our own bundle of joy?" He asks poking at her belly.

A few months ago Jazzman would have gotten all flushed with joy hearing that from him, but somehow now she is not as thrilled. She finds a way to mask her emotions, "Marriage first, then comes baby. I'm selfish. I want to enjoy quality time with you first, like right now." She whispers in his ear, "You see that door behind you?"

Afrique nods his head yes.

She continues, "I want you to tell the guard that I have your permission to go in there. I will meet you there in five minutes. Do you think you can do that for me?" She is playing with him, pretending to be him the first night they met in Miami.

They both laugh and walk into his dressing room. As soon as the door closes behind them Jazzman begins to seduce him with her love. Her lustful, heating body begs for him to cure her anxiety. She's been sexually deprived and needs him to fulfill her every desire with his touch as he strokes in and out making her feel pleasure.

She too pleases her man as a reminder of what he has waiting for him at home. Her tongue captures every inch of his naked flesh and he reacts with his hands caressing her body letting her know he wants more. This night is all about Afrique. She wants him to know that once in a while she is okay with taking control and tonight he fell witness to another side of Jazzman.

By the time she finishes communicating with her body, juices are flowing, feelings of satisfaction are in the air. She accomplishes what she set forth to do, handle her business with the end result, sexing him and leaving him with those thoughts.

As soon as it is over, she is on the next plane back to Miami, leaving him to fall in love with her all over again. Like Kim would say, "yuh sort dat out rude girl style…signed…sealed…done!"

Jazzman feels like this had to be done. She does not want to assume the worst of Afrique, but if he is starting to catch feelings for another woman, she wants to shut it down with her presence.

The next day he is calling her to find out when she will do it again. The encounter has him craving her. He wants more of that, because it suppresses his loneliness while on tour. Yet for Jazzman, her actions mask her uneasy state of mind.

$$\infty$$

NEW YORK CITY, NY
Afrique

The next morning, Afrique is reading the New York Times, enjoying breakfast on the patio after his night with Jazzman. He laughs at the newspaper comments insinuating that he and Diamond might have something going on. It's times like these he is grateful that he has a secure woman in his life.

When he hears a knock at the door, instantly he hopes Jazzman has come back for more. His smile turns upside down when he looks through the peephole and sees Diamond. He lets her in.

"Good mornin'. Have you recovered from last night?" Afrique asks going back to the patio.

"I think I should be asking you that same question." Diamond follows close behind sitting opposite of him.

Afrique responds with a huge grin, "Any time I see my woman it's a good day."

"Yuh nuh say! If yah ask me, I tink your woman is feelin a likkle insecure. She worried dat yuh might wrap your hands around my body—" She pauses unsure if she should say her next comment, but she does since she feels comfortable around him. "—And me give you some of my punani?"

They both glance at one another and bust out laughing.

Afrique says, "Yah mad."

Diamond tries to sound cheerful, "How come she didn't stick around? It would have been nice to catch up with her. Are things cool between you two?"

Afrique puts his paper down questioning, "Yuh good?"

"Yah, why you ask?" Diamond responds with curiosity.

Afrique stares directly at Diamond answering, "Don't worry about my woman. She good! My life with Jazzman is none of your business."

She agrees, "Yuh right! So let's talk about us. I really like you, yuh know. I tink you and I can make great music together. The reviews we received from last night's performance and from the skit we did together, I think confirms it. That moment we shared on stage was filled with chemistry. I think the audience felt it, too."

"Look, you are beautiful and talented, but you are my opening act. That's it."

Diamond replies with a smirk on her face. "Correction...I'm just your opening act right now, but things will change."

"I have Jazzman and I'm good! I'm not going to mess up tings with her, yuh understand?" Afrique's eyes connect with hers to assert his position.

"She is not all that innocent yuh know. You keep tinkin yuh have da golden prize. Hold on, is it Oriba the one that wants her? Haven't they been in the studio working on an album? Or is it her partner in crime? What's his name...oh yah, Tyson. He wants her! Those two belong together, just like you and I belong together."

Afrique can't believe this woman is getting under his skin. He also can't believe what she is saying, because Jazzman has not mentioned studio time with Oriba. To add to his frustration, every time he hears Tyson's name in connection with Jazzman, it infuriates him.

Diamond can tell she found his weak spot when he says, "I think it's time for you to go."

Diamond says, "Remember the words to our song, if you need me, check fi me. As a newcomer I hear it gets really lonely on tour." When she gets up he glances over at her backside and notices she is not wearing panties from the way her dress is sucked into the crease of her cheeks.

She turns back and tilts her head down to whisper in his ear, "If you need someone to keep yuh warm at night mi only a few doors away. I wouldn't mind yuh buddy slippin inside me." She strokes his bicep with her fingers and slowly turns away making sure her ass is leveled with his eyes. She exaggerates her movements as she sways her hips from side to side, providing a hint of temptation to Afrique. Her walk seems to say that her body is worth pursuing. As her little cotton dress caresses her body, he finds his mind wandering briefly as he imagines what her dress is hiding. His second head piques interest and it becomes a close call for Afrique. He shakes his head quickly, dismissing these thoughts. Instead, he thinks of Jazzman's recent visit and the excitement he feels when he is with her.

He is certain that pre-Jazzman he would have been all over it, banging Diamond the moment he got off stage. He knows his commitment is to Jazzman, but had she not come into town to see him, he's not sure if he would have slipped up. This brings him to the realization that staying with one woman is going to be harder than he thought, especially having so many offers with no strings attached.

MIAMI, FL
Jazzman & Afrique

[BAM!]

Jazzman slams the magazine on her desk. She is fuming from reading the reviews indicating that Afrique and Diamond complement each other very well on and off stage. It indicates their chemistry is igniting. It also insinuates that the two could be more than music partners and living according to the lyrics of their duet. Apparently they have a new song, "Check Fi Me," about a love affair, a man cheating on his wife. Afrique failed to mention anything when she saw him on Saturday, but then again she wasn't there long enough to uncover the 411. They performed the song for the first time this past weekend and it's been getting great reviews. It infuriates her that she is finding out through a magazine article and not her man. She knows if it were another female artist collaborating with Afrique it would be no big deal to her. But being Diamond, it is seeping into her skin, like a bad rash that won't go away. What makes it worse is that everyone loves Diamond.

Jazzman wonders, *Maybe it makes sense, the reason why he didn't go to Miami to spend time with Desmond. It has to do with the song. I wonder if his weekend detour in Jamaica was studio time with Diamond, which would mean they were probably working on this for some time prior. Why the big secret? Why not tell me?*

Jazzman knew this would constantly be on her mind if she did not find out soon what was up. She is not even sure how to ask Afrique as she dials his hotel room. She is relieved when he picks up, "Hey baby, how are you? How was your performance?"

He answers with not much enthusiasm, "Hey, Jazz. It was good."

"Are you okay?" She's not used to hearing him like this.

"No, I'm not!" Afrique puts down a local newspaper that he just finished reading. It was a review that criticized his performance. He is beginning to feel the same madness he felt during his conversation with Diamond.

"What's wrong? Can I help?" Jazzman tries to sound cheerful even though she is upset about what she read. She wonders if the tabloids are getting to him, too.

"You can help by telling me why you failed to mention your studio time with Oriba?" Afrique gets even more upset as he says the words out loud.

"You got to be kidding me right now. Really? Are you kidding me right now?" Jazzman is dumbfounded with his questioning, because being in the studio with Oriba should be no big deal.

"Yah, I'm dead serious." Afrique knows the real anger comes from what he just read, but he also wonders if Tyson has been in the studio with her.

"I guess I forgot just like you failed to mention your studio time with Diamond. Oh that's right, she was more important than spending time with your son. You got some nerve right now. Have a good show tonight. That's what I called to tell you." Jazzman hangs up before he could reply or defend himself. She is not in the mood to hear his excuses, especially with the recent tabloids insinuating an affair. She takes a deep breath and continues reading the article so she can feel justified in hanging up on him. However, she is shocked when she reads the critique on Afrique's performance. He received a bad review. She feels horrible for hanging up, but not sorry for standing her ground by speaking her mind.

Afrique can't believe Jazzman just hung up on him. However, it's clear to him that she is upset about Diamond. He wonders how she found out about the studio time. He's uncertain if someone told her something or if she just read the articles that have been written. He's tired of reporters starting rumors. He knows if he were in her shoes he would feel like he was being played. It's how he feels right now. He feels guilty for attacking her instead of just getting to the root of his other concern, Tyson.

MIAMI, FL
Jazzman and Oriba

Jazzman is not in the mood for office gossip, knowing that the recent articles might lead to various assumptions. Feeling the stress growing, she decides to head out to the studio. She drops off some paperwork for her assistant to handle and lets her know she will be at the studio with Oriba.

It's moments like these, when situations leave her feeling out of control and mad at the world, that she really appreciates her job for being a diversion. She can block out the negative feelings and channel her energy into getting her job done well.

The fresh air hits her as she gets out of her car and walks into the studio. It calms her current state of mind, knowing the hours ahead will take her mind off the situation with Afrique.

When she opens the door to Oriba's studio, he calls out to her through the microphone with a smile on his face, "Jazzman, I wasn't expecting to see you today."

Jazzman reciprocates the smile, feeling the love. Pressing the intercom button she replies, "What's up? Somehow working at the office was not as exciting as hitting the studio. I need some positive energy and this place seems like the perfect spot."

Oriba gets out of the booth to give her a hug.

Jazzman gives him a tight squeeze saying, "Don't let me stop you from doing your thing."

"Actually, I'm glad you're here. I want you to hear this track we finished a couple of hours ago. Jay, can you key it up for Jazz?"

Jay presses a few buttons. "It's all set. I'm going to grab some breakfast. Do either of you want anything?"

"I'm all set." Jazzman responds pointing to her cup of coffee.

Oriba responds, "I'm good."

As soon as Jay walks out, Oriba pulls up a chair next to Jazzman. Before he starts the track he asks, "So, what have you been up to, anything exciting?"

"I had to leave town to see Afrique."

"How was it?"

Jazzman, lost in her thoughts for a few seconds appears confused, "How was what?"

He explains, "Your visit with Afrique, the big concert. I heard about it. I'm assuming you went to that performance."

"Oh, sorry. It was really nice. Thank you for asking." As she responds her facial expression changes. Although she doesn't realize it, Oriba sees the look of sadness that flashes across her face.

Oriba wants to press her for additional information, but he decides the best thing to do is press the play button and let the words of the song speak for him.

The song begins with the sound of a heartbeat in slow motion which sends Jazzman's heart racing. She is unclear as to why her body begins to react so soon to the melody when the words to the song have yet to begin. The beat pumps up to a beautiful rhythm. The guitar mixed with the piano intrigues her. She listens closely as the words to the song begin to tell a story. A story of a man who loves his woman and although he knows he should not cheat, his love for 'women' far exceeds his need to do the right thing. Sharing a piece of his love with every fine thing gives him great pleasure, yet he is trying to hang on to the woman who will be there for him at any cost. So he questions why he can't do the same in return.

At the end of the song Oriba asks, "What do you think?"

The lyrics encourage her to evaluate her own life. "It's hot! It's a hit record, no doubt."

Oriba smiles, "You think?"

"I think? I know and feel it! That one is a hit. What else are you working on?"

Oriba is excited, "I'm working on this club joint that I want you to hear and I need your feedback."

"Hit it!" Jazzman sits back in her chair.

Come to me (Come to me)
When you need some good lovin'
Come to me (Come to me)
Move your hips in my direction
Come to me (Come to me)
Cause I need your sexy ass wrapped around my body

While the instrumental section is playing, Oriba says, "This part needs words and I'm not sure what to put here." After the instrumental section, the chorus is heard again.

Come to me (Come to me)
When your night gets lonely
Come to me (Come to me)
Give me that good lovin'
Come to me (Come to me)
Let your lips touch my body

Oriba stops the music. "That's what I have so far and I'm stuck. I'm not sure where to go from there."

"Wow, I like what you have so far...hmm...give me a few minutes, my mind is racing and I don't want to lose my train of thought."

"Cool, I'm going to grab some water. Want some?"

"Sure."

As Oriba walks out, Jazzman begins jotting down lyrics. She plays the melody one more time to make sure the words flow with the beat.

When Oriba returns ten minutes later he asks, "Are you good?"

"Yes, the whole time I was flirting with some words. I have an idea. I want to know what you think."

"I'm open to whatever. This song has me stuck, but it has potential."

"I'm thinking we juice it up with Reggaeton, add a few Spanish words to the song, we give it a crossover effect and we can test the market with this one. I think it's hot...a club joint for sure." Jazzman looks in his direction to sense his vibe, but the idea is not sparking an interest from what she can read on his facial expression.

Jazzman adds, "How about this...you take a break...you look like you can use one—" She waits for his reaction, "—that was a joke."

They both start laughing and she continues, "So, take a break. Go for a walk on the beach or grab a tea or coffee. I'm going to the office to pick up some samples and we meet back here in an hour. How does that sound?"

"Cool, but I'm not crazy about your idea. I just want you to know that!"

"I hear you, but keep an open mind. It's all I ask."

Jazzman walks with Oriba to the parking lot, and when he drives away she goes back to the studio. She asks the receptionist if Destin, a Reggaeton producer, is still in the studio. She's happy to hear he is, and she tracks him down to ask him to meet her in Oriba's studio in a half hour.

Jazzman goes to work on the song, keying up the music to recap and feel what she wrote. She experiments with the beat as well, quickly changing her mind and leaving that part to the professional. She decides to modify the lyrics, knowing it is going to be a hard sell. Her adrenaline rush is pumping since her time is limited. She lives for times like this. It's an out-of-body experience when her creativity blossoms.

She adds the beat and plays it again to make sure it flows.

Destin walks in at the right time. She explains her version and what she envisions for the song. Destin takes a few minutes to collect his thoughts and sends Jazzman to the recording booth to add the female lyrics. Destin pulls his artist, Chino, into the studio for the male lyrics. They go through a couple of takes to make it flow so that by the time Oriba returns to the studio the song's real potential is obvious.

As they play back the song, Destin, Chino and Jazzman are rockin' to the beat. It's that kind of jam the body can't help but move, creating a dance floor anywhere the song is playing.

When Oriba walks in after his break he asks, "What's up? What a gwan?"

Jazzman blushes feeling caught with her hands in the cookie jar. "Welcome back. This is Destin, a Reggaeton producer, and his artist, Chino. Remember when I said lets take a break?"

He gives them both dap and says, "Yah-"

"Well, I stayed and tried something. See what you think." Jazzman plays the song for Oriba.

The reggae beat is wicked with the emphasis on the second and fourth beat, seasoning it with the Reggaeton beat causing cultures to blend into a beautiful mixed marriage. As he listens to the variation of the male and female vocals in Spanish, he realizes this could be what the song needs. He has no clue what they were saying, but he loves the sound and the beat. The melody mixed with the words piques his curiosity as to the meaning of the lyrics. At the end of the song that's his first question. Jazzman explains 'cojelo suave' is to take it slow and 'damelo duro' is to give it hard. Oriba sits back for a few minutes, thinking, and then goes right to work laying the track and adding even more lyrics to the song.

After a long day of work they sit back to hear their creation in its entirety:

HOW DOES IT FEEL

ORIBA
Come to me (Come to me)
When you need some good lovin'
Come to me (Come to me)
Move your hips in my direction
Come to me (Come to me)
When you need some affection

Touch me…Touch me…Put your lips pon my body (male vocals)
Talk to me…Talk to me…Tell me if I'm getting warma (female vocals)

Cojelo Suave, mami (male vocals)
Cojelo…Cojelo (female vocals)
Nice and Slow (Oriba)
Damelo duro, papi (female vocals)
Damelo…Damelo (male vocals)

You feel me, Mami (Oriba)
Cojelo…Cojelo (female vocals)

When I see you on the dance floor (Oriba)
Damelo…Damelo (female vocals)

ORIBA
Come to me (Come to me)
When you need some good lovin'
Come to me (Come to me)
Move your hips in my direction
Come to me (Come to me)
When you need some affection

Touch me…Touch me…Put your lips pon my body (male vocals)
Talk to me…Talk to me…Tell me if I'm getting warma (female vocals)

Cojelo Suave, mami (male vocals)
Cojelo…Cojelo (female vocals)
Nice and Slow (Oriba)
Damelo duro, papi (female vocals)
Damelo…Damelo (male vocals)

You feel me, Mami (Oriba)
Cojelo…Cojelo (female vocals)
Tell me how you like it (Oriba)
Damelo…Damelo (female vocals)

You feel me…You feel me…(female vocals)
HOW-DOES-IT-FEEL? (Oriba)

They decide to keep Jazzman's voice in the song, at least for now, but they agree some more takes are necessary for fine-tuning. To lock the song in place, Jazzman checks in with her boss for approval. Charles makes an appearance at the studio to give his blessing.

When the studio clears, Jazzman and Oriba are the only two left. As the sun goes down, they light candles to allow some more creativity to flow. They work on lyrics to an instrumental melody provided by Jay, the engineer. As they continue writing more lyrics it's clear their chemistry in the studio is undeniable. They agree to hold two of the songs they created and release them as singles, after the album release, to generate additional cash flow. Their connection allows Oriba to trust Jazzman with his career. He begins to sense that she has his best interest at heart and is feeling confident that she will keep his creativity intact when completing the album.

After a long day of work, she asks him to play the song she listened to when she first walked into the studio. She forgot some of the words, but she remembers the effect it had on her. He queues the song, so she can burn a copy. They allow the music to play as they silently listen, and when she hears the chorus she feels goose bumps.

Here I go again, living a double life
Telling her she is the only one
Only woman I call wife
How do I confess, the true meaning of my strife
A man like me just needs a few
A few women to make life nice
When I tell her she is the only one
I wonder, why she buys my lies

It's a woman's shape and those hips
The way they sway from east to west
It's the shape of her lips
The way her tongue wets them from side to side
It's a woman's soulful eyes…her beautiful smile
How can I resist her look and her style

As the song plays, she wonders if Oriba knows something about Afrique. Given her knowledge of the music business, she can't help but to wonder if Afrique is playing her. She does not want to feel either rejected or played. She recognizes the risk she takes being involved with a famous musician who is often away on the road with temptation always around. She is tired of not feeling 'good enough'. She is still haunted by what she feels from her father's rejection.

She silently begins to cry and does not even realize it until the end of the song when Oriba suddenly asks, "Are you okay?"

As she wipes away the tears she responds, "I'm okay. I guess your song has that much of an affect on me."

"Do you think women are going to hate me because of the cheating thing?" Oriba asks, wondering if Jazzman will open up.

"Well, the song is reality. It speaks truth and some people can handle truth while others are not ready for it. Some people don't want to see the problems in their relationship. They are more comfortable with a bad situation, pretending its love when it's a façade. I'm sorry. I didn't mean to get philosophical on you, but to sum it up, a little controversy never hurts. In fact it may make the song an even bigger hit."

"You okay, Jazz? It seems like you're here, but your mind is somewhere else."

"No, I'm good." Jazzman responds while looking through her purse to hide the emotions visible from her expression.

"You keep saying that, so I'm just going to come out with it. Is everything okay with Afrique?"

"Why do you ask?" She is defensive now.

He responds, "I read the tabloids too, you know. Let's just say it's hard to believe a man with Afrique's past reputation would just change his ways for love especially while still living the lifestyle of a musician."

Irritated, Jazzman quickly responds, "Really? Who are you to judge? I don't see you getting 'man of the year' award." Then she stops herself and continues calmly, "Anyway, I really enjoyed my time with you today and I don't want to end it on a bad note. Lets just leave this conversation unfinished, okay? So, this is goodnight." Jazzman gets up to walk out.

Oriba reaches for her and says, "I'm sorry, Jazz. Maybe I stepped out of line. It just seems like you were dealing with something and I wanted to see if I could help."

"No, you're right in a way. I think your song struck a chord, but I'm okay."

"Really, I'm sorry! So, are we good?" He reaches out for a hug, Jazzman slightly hugs him, wanting to rush out to get some fresh air. She has a lot to think about and her head is pounding. She is unsure of how to make sense of the conversation, wondering in spite of herself how much of what he had said is really true.

He continues, "Yuh beautiful and I just want you to be happy. All I'm saying, word on the street is 'what Diamond wants, Diamond gets'. Just be careful. I don't want to see you get hurt. I'm glad I got to make you smile today. I can see you needed some cheering up. What I just said, is how I should have started this conversation. I do that sometimes...I speak before I think. Remember, I can be an ass sometimes." Oriba's tone is extremely apologetic.

Jazzman smiles and says with a slight laugh, "I know. Actually, I think all men can be asses sometimes! That's why I have you signed up for some classes. I want to make sure you don't make an ass of yourself or the label. The BIG time is no joke and I want you to be ready when it hits. You're going places and I want those places to be stardom and the top of the charts."

"Classes...what classes?"

"Personal development classes. Oh yeah and maybe a class on when to say things and when to hold your tongue! My secretary will let you know the days. Have a good night!" Jazzman smiles feeling like she got the last laugh, not intentionally, but it felt good since he just gave her the beginning of a headache.

Unsure if she is serious or just playing with him, he's left feeling like he received the worst news ever. "Yah, good night."

She walks outside and the pounding in her head intensifies, filled with thoughts of one question. *Is there something going on between Afrique and Diamond? Is it chemistry? Is it just a publicity stunt or* is it her overactive imagination and insecurities getting the best of her. And if so, why doesn't Afrique say anything about it? All these thoughts run through her mind as she gets into her car, feeling like she needs an aspirin or a drink. Maybe both!

Chapter 9

HARTFORD, CT
Afrique and Diamond

[CHEERS]

"HARTFORD CONNECTICUT YUH READY FOR ME TO CHECK FI YUH?" As the crowd cheers louder, Diamond smiles. "YUH NUH WANT IT?" She smiles for a moment to take in the cheers that are for her. "I SAID CONNECTICUT ARE YOU READY FOR AFRIQUE?" The crowd cheers even louder and the lights turn off. Diamond laughs into the microphone. Then the spotlight is on her body movements blending with the beat. After a few minutes, the spotlight turns off and the music stops.

Diamond flicks on her lighter and says, "I'M GONNA TRY DIS ONE MORE TIME CONNECTICUT! CONNECTICUT…YUH READY FOR AFRIQUE TO MASH IT UP WHEN HE CUM PON DI STAGE AND CHECK FI ME?" Once again, the crowd expresses their excitement as it grows pitch black. When the music fades up simultaneously with the spotlight, Afrique is right up on Diamond grinding her to the beat of the music. The crowd goes wild.

Afrique shouts, "Connecticut, I hear dat woman want us men to rub dem…inject dem body wid some wicked lovin' just like dis." They both sensually touch each other to the beat.

Diamond makes a correction, "Not me...Not Diamond...I like it rough."

The crowd flicks on their lighters and shouts, "Pram!! Pram!!"

She says to Afrique, "Yuh hear dat? Give it to me how Connecticut like it...Rough!"

"So, yuh wan me fi beat it up?"

The audience yells various blurbs, "Bumba! Bullet! Bullet!"

"Give me buddy, just like dat! Cause a womon like me get lonely pon da road ...yuh know—" Diamond begins to sing a cappella, "—Check for me...Check fi me...a man like you knows how to touch me...sex me through da night."

The music starts up again and they continue their performance, singing together:

Diamond
When I'm alone
Laying in my bed
(Check fi me...Check fi me)
I toss and turn
With thoughts of you in my head
(Check fi me...Check fi me)
Wondering when you'll leave her
And slip into my bed
(Check fi me...Check fi me)

Afrique
F-E-L-L-A-Z...We Run Tings

~

Wife and matte is how Jamaicans dweet
I mus proceed with caution
Wifey find mi, it may cause disruption
Dis is risky business
Fellaz you get the action

<u>Diamond</u>
If her lovin' was good yuh no be wid me
<u>Afrique</u>
Me no say dat…Yuh trouble and mi like dat
<u>Female Background Vocals</u>
Yuh play wid fire yah gonna get burned

<u>Afrique</u>
Corruption in bed
(Check fi me…Check fi me)
Proceed with caution
(Check fi me…Check fi me)
Yuh play wid fire
(Check fi me…check fi me)
Work my body
(Check fi me…Check fi me)

<u>Diamond</u>
Yuh have the right tool to fix it
<u>Afrique</u>
You have da right glue to wuk my body
<u>Afrique</u>
I'll take control like a Nascar driver
<u>Diamond</u>
Hose me down like a firefighter

As they continue on stage singing, the tension of wanting esca-
lates. They want to finish what they start on stage behind closed
doors. Each time they perform this song, it heightens the tension
between them and the attraction. They understand one another and
can relate to feelings of loneliness on the road.

On this night, Diamond has a trick up her sleeve, because she
can't deal with another rejection from Afrique. When the crew goes
out to dinner, her date will be the Regional Sales Manager, Chris,

from Hot 93.7 – a local radio station. She knows putting another guy in the mix will make Afrique jealous and intensify his craving.

During dinner she is glowing with all the attention she is receiving. She is loving every minute of it.

When they get back to the hotel, Diamond doesn't enter her room alone and she makes sure Afrique knows about it. After all she is a woman with needs and she has to fulfill them even if it's not with the guy she has her eyes on. To her surprise she is pleased with Chris's performance. His tongue is obsessed with her body, and he injects it with a temporary cure. He whispers all the right things in her ear to pump up her ego and shocks her body with intense excitement. When her juices begin to surface, she saddles up and rocks him into complete satisfaction. When it is all said and done, she decides to keep him on her list for future hook-ups.

The next night, it is obvious Afrique wants what he can't have and it is killing him. He is in a committed relationship and he convinces himself each night that ruining a good thing is not worth the risk. Although, there is that other voice inside him that says she won't find out, if he is careful. Then, his senses bring him back to reality, remembering that being single with different women every night is a rush, but really getting to know one woman gives him a sense of purpose in his life.

Jazzman understands him and she allows him to do his thing. She is not clingy and has her own life. Thinking about her and the connection they share is enough to dismiss any temptation on making a move with Diamond. He has a good thing for the first time and he is not about to let temptation ruin their relationship. He feels safe tonight having talked himself out of a sticky situation, but he knows this is a reoccurring temptation. He will have to play the same mental game with himself.

MIAMI, FL
Jazzman

"Bye!" Jazzman walks out of therapy feeling energized. She feels better equipped to make important decisions about things that impact her personally. She knows she will still need help along the way, like accepting things she can't control, which makes her feel uncomfortable. She discovers that never saying no to her mother has spilled over to her relationship with Afrique. It's the reason she still feels like crap for telling him she will consider moving to Jamaica. She aims to please, so saying no will sometimes feel uncomfortable, but she knows she must in order to be true to herself. Learning to say no is her new assignment before her next appointment with Helen.

When she gets back to the office there is a message from Afrique.

She returns the call finding him extremely concerned. "Hey babe, are you okay?"

She is confused, "Yes, why wouldn't I be?"

"Your assistant said you were at a doctor's appointment and I don't remember you telling me you had one. So I've been worried. Why were you at the doctors? Are you pregnant?"

Jazzman grows a little heated that her assistant would tell him that much information and upset that she has to tell him the truth about something she wants to keep private at the moment, "No, I've been seeing a therapist." She grows even more mad now, at herself for saying it that way. Now, he'll know she has been more than one time.

"Therapy? Why? What kind of foolishness is that? You don't need therapy. You seem fine to me. Besides I don't think you should be going to therapy. People will be stereotyping you as crazy and I don't want anyone labeling my woman crazy."

She can tell by the tone of his voice that he is mad.

Afrique continues, "I'm calling you to apologize and now I find out you have been keeping a secret like this from me. Looks like this is something else you failed to mention. Seems like lately you are forgetting to tell me a lot of things. Yet, you want to get on my case. You must be mad."

She calmly replies not wanting to argue, "It's not like that. I just want to go to these appointments and figure some things out without all the interrogation."

He is livid. "Oh, so you are basically telling me had your assistant not accidently told me you were at a doctor's appointment, I would be in the dark right now. WOW!"

She calmly states again, "It's not like that."

Afrique gives his opinion whether she wants it or not. "Well, let me tell you what it's like. I do not agree with you going to therapy. I don't agree with talking to some stranger about your problems when you should be talking to me. By the way, why are you seeing a therapist?"

She is in shock that he has no clue why she would be going, "Let's see, my mom passed away to cancer. My dad hasn't been present in my life since I was a little girl. And my man is 'feeling-up' another woman on stage every day of the week."

Afrique grows even more agitated; "You are kidding me right now. You want to put this on me. I don't think so. It doesn't work like that. Besides, had you listened to me about us moving to Jamaica and starting our life there, we would not be having these problems right now."

"Oh really! How would being in Jamaica change any of this? Besides, I didn't know we were having problems. I thought we were just having a disagreement. Thank you for clarifying. Listen, I have to go into a meeting. We can talk about this later."

"Ya, lata." He hangs up feeling like she is lying about needing to go into a meeting and questioning the state of their relationship.

Jazzman can't believe he hung up on her, and the things he expressed to her. It brought her back to her self-discovery at therapy today. She had explained to her therapist that her body responds when someone says something to her that does not feel right. Jazzman calls it one of her pressure points. She gets a sensation in the pit of her stomach when a situation like this occurs. She feels uncomfortable with his perspective regarding her therapy. She feels judged and it bothers her. Their conversation leaves her with more doubts about the relationship and how to fix it. She does not like feeling upset especially with Afrique being so far away. She's worried their argument will leave the door wide open for the hoochie mamas.

⌒♾

MIAMI, FL
Jazzman and Kim

After work and before pole dancing class Jazzman meets up with Kim for coffee. Their lives have been so busy that they barely have time for one another. So, after ordering their coffee they walk outside to find a table with an umbrella on this rainy Miami day.

Jazzman feels as gloomy as the day. She has so much to get off her chest but first things first. "How have you been? How are things with Rick?"

The spark in Kim's eyes says it all. "I've been extremely busy at work and things with Rick are perfect. We are still getting to know one another. This is the first relationship that is going slow and I'm enjoying it. It doesn't feel rushed like all the other relationships I've been in. We take turns visiting one another and we are enjoying that right now. He's such a great guy; I think he might be the one. We are nowhere near that, of course. If we cross that bridge, we will have to decide on NYC or Miami."

"I'm so happy for you Kim. You deserve it. You've had your share of heartbreakers so I'm happy that you have Rick. He compliments you well."

"Thank you. I'm just glad I changed my mind that day in P.R. and said yes. He's been heaven-sent and I'm not taking this relationship for granted. Enough about me, how are things with you?"

The look on Jazzman's face says it all, she needs a friend to talk to. "Kim, it's been rough. I can't stand that Afrique is on tour with Diamond."

"That has to be so hard to deal with. You know I'm usually rooting for Afrique, but this one I have to admit, is a tough pill to swallow." Kim takes a sip of coffee.

"I'm not managing it well at all. It's constantly on my mind, because we know how Diamond gets down. I have my own stuff that I'm dealing with and this has BAD written all over it." Jazzman takes a sip of coffee, "So there is something I need to get off my chest. Well, you know I surprised him with a visit and that was great! What I didn't like was the way Diamond was invading his personal space. Before I could observe any further his camp shouted 'what's up' as I was approaching. Diamond walked away when she saw me, and I didn't question Afrique about it. I was pissed, but I brushed it aside to be my cheerful self for Afrique. To make a long story short, I gave it to him rude girl style. I left him fulfilled and wanting more of me so he would not be tempted else where."

Kim raises her hand for a high five, "That's my girl!"

Jazzman giggles and raises her hand to connect with Kim's. "But get a load of this…I find out from the tabloids that he has a duet with Diamond. I called him yesterday to find out why he didn't tell me, but I didn't get a chance to ask him. He was pissed off at me for being in the studio with Oriba. Can you believe it? That's my bread and butter."

"That's weird, Jazz. Why would he do that? It doesn't sound right. Maybe there is something else going on with him. He's never been the type to question your work, except when it comes to Tyson, but that's a given. I don't know!" Kim is surprised at Afrique's reaction.

"That's not all! He tried to call me today when I was at therapy and my assistant told him I was at a doctor's appointment. I was pissed that she said that. Well, when I called him back I had to tell him about therapy. Now he's upset that I didn't tell him about that. He also had the nerve to say I shouldn't be going. He said he doesn't want anyone labeling his WOMAN as crazy." Jazzman waits for Kim's reaction.

She gives her the look she is expecting. "Are you serious? I can't imagine being in your position, but at the same time he shouldn't have said that to you. You don't deserve that. However, the Jamaican in me will tell you that it's not part of our culture, Jazz. Therapy is one of those things we Blacks and Ricans don't do."

"And I get that. I guess that's why he said it's foolishness." Jazzman gives Kim that eye and they both start laughing. Jamaicans are quick to label American customs as 'foolishness' when they feel it's a stupid idea. "But all joking aside, when I told Tyson he was happy for me. He even offered to go with me, and yet Afrique, the man I'm supposed to marry, doesn't even support me on something that I really need right now. It stinks."

"I'm sorry."

"Thank you. I just can't believe my life right now. When it rains it pours with Afrique."

"Jazz, I hope you don't get offended when I say this, but any one-night stands I have had...never ended well. It's hard for something to grow from that type of situation. I know your circumstance with Afrique is different, but there are other things to take into consideration. He is constantly on tour. His determination to stay monogamous can be manageable, yet it can be extremely difficult."

Jazzman sadly responds, "I hear you, girl,"

"Sounds like we need another vacation. What do you say?" Kim exposes her smile hoping Jazzman reciprocates.

"I'd love to, but I can't. Let's revisit that plan after I get back from New Orleans. Right now I feel like I need some 'me time' with my thoughts. I'm at a crossroad and I'm going to have to weigh my pros and cons. This sucks." The thought of saying she can't go to class today crosses her mind. She is not in the mood to go, but she knows Kim won't have it. She has visions of her face caressing the pillow and falling asleep. However, getting her 'sexy' on and forgetting Afrique for the moment sounds good, too.

135

"I know it sucks. Well, you should pray on it...that usually helps you. Do you want to talk some more or are you ready to go?"

"Let's go get our freak on!"

⌒〇

MIAMI, FL
Jazzman and Kim

"Now that you ladies have been taking my class for several weeks, I want to talk to you about what drives us as women in the bedroom. For us to get turned on there is no magic pill. The key to exciting us is our happiness. In other words, our sexual pleasures are hidden in the things we enjoy doing. For some women, particularly mothers, it's important to have work-life balance, scheduling time for work and family. But there is a part that is overlooked, time for self. It's important to have hobbies, passions, reading a book that gets you in the mood or a movie of your choice, etc. Doctors also say we need the sun to keep us in good spirits. Think about it...don't you feel sexy after some time laying out in the sun or at the beach?" Lindsey says this as she stretches her body in a sensual way, and the women in the class follow her lead. They are all in agreement.

Lindsey continues, "Imagine northerners who have the winter months to deal with, many dreary days with little sun during those months. We are lucky to have sun and nice weather all year round. What sexual frustration must exist in those states, except for New York, of course. I'm sure New York makes up for the uptight people lacking sexual healing in Northern America." All the women laugh and nod in agreement, except for Jazzman. Her stomach knots up at the thought of Tyson in New York with all those beautiful, confident women.

Kim laughs and continues to smile thinking of the excitement New York has brought into her life emotionally and sexually.

Elizabeth adds, "Don't forget D.C. – You know those politicians, they need to release the tension of the world."

The women laugh again.

"Okay ladies, your time has come and I hope you are all ready. When I begin to play the music I want one of you to get up and entertain us. Pretend we are your significant other and release. After your routine, find an interesting way to tag our next entertainer. Do not hold back!"

One by one the ladies open up and their insecurities begins to disappear, as their confidence begins to fragrance the air. Through their touch, their hands caress the pole. Their bodies twirl around it and some perform the butterfly move and some manage with the firefighter slide. Several of the women enhance their performance by touching their own bodies and others strike a passionate pose from time to time. The women were transforming before Lindsey's eyes. They are not the timid women that first entered her class.

Each woman performs using what she has learned during strip-tease class. They take it slow, make their goods pop and bring it down low. They have fun with their performances and it shows as they each have their own signature move.

Now they know, that a man's hungry eyes will wait for the prize as long as he gets it once it's exposed. They know the routine will bring excitement to the bedroom and they will enjoy slipping on a pair of stilettos that scream, "I'm going to be out of control tonight."

For these women taking their clothes off for their partner will never be the same. They have transformed into sensual women and in the bedroom they will move to a different tune with the lights on. As Lindsey says, "Lights on, move slow, let the passion guide your flow!"

MIAMI, FL
Jazzman

Jazzman unlocks the door to her home. It feels empty without Afrique and she wishes he were welcoming her home. She also wouldn't mind welcoming him home after a long day at work, but that is not the lifestyle they live. Their lifestyle is glamorous, but quite lonely. She so desperately would like to release and make love to him using the techniques she performed at pole dancing class today.

By the same token, Afrique's behavior has her questioning their love. She wonders if it can withstand hard times and if he can handle her therapy sessions. She presses play on the answering machine to listen to her messages. Apparently it's already too much, a message from Afrique indicates he will not be in Miami this weekend.

Jazzman still can't get over her conversation with him. She also can't believe that she yelled at her assistant for informing Afrique she had a doctor's appointment. She replays in her head what she screamed, *next time you keep that shit private! If that shit goes down again, you will find yourself without a job!* She reacted in a manner that she had sworn would never be her style. She has always hated how some executives in the industry talk to their employees, and that's exactly how she behaved today. Employees usually put up with it because in the entertainment industry, you put up and shut up. She knew she was out of line and it was her own fault for not informing Afrique about therapy. She ended up apologizing to her assistant before she left for the day.

Now she finds herself alone and torn between two worlds, unclear which is the best path to travel. She decides to go for a walk on the beach to help clear her mind and sort through her thoughts.

Before heading out, she opens her bible for some spiritual guidance. She flips to Philippians Chapter 4, Verses 8 – 9:

> "Finally, beloved, whatever is true, whatever is honorable, whatever is just, whatever is pure, whatever is pleasing, whatever is commendable, if there is any excellence and if there is anything worthy of praise, think about these things. Keep on doing the things that you have learned and received and heard and seen in me, and the God of peace will be with you."

This scripture motivates her every time she is going through a difficult time in her career or has to make major decisions in her life.

As she begins her walk, she gets a sense of déjà vu, realizing she was doing this same thing a couple of months ago when she was on vacation with Afrique. Here she is again questioning their relationship. These thoughts bring on a migraine. Just like the ones she gets right after therapy from too many thoughts rushing to be released in a forty-five minute session.

Although she's been through a lot of trials and tribulations with Afrique she feels that it's a testament to what their relationship can withstand. Or is it? This is the question that has her at a crossroads. She has played it in her head until it has become a broken record. Now, she has new concerns and it's due to seeing a side of Afrique she has never known. She never thought for one second he would question her work or question her going to therapy. She needs someone to support her, not put her down and she needs to feel secure about her relationship. Lately, she is not getting either one from Afrique.

She also questions if it's her own doing. Any time she has a problem, she goes to Tyson. Any time she needs to make choices in life, she bounces her ideas off Tyson. Any time she needs a friend she goes to Tyson.

As she is walking, she says to herself, *One thing's for sure, my best friend is leaving soon. Maybe once he leaves my relationship with Afrique will be back on track. Maybe it will help Afrique to see he has nothing to worry about. That feels right! Finally something good comes out of Tyson moving to New York. First things first...I need to schedule another trip to surprise my man. It will be just what the doctor ordered. I do not want all the moves I learned in pole dancing class to go to waste. I'm ready to drop it like it's hot for my man. I want him to have my name exploding in his mind all day and night.*

She giggles and continues thinking to herself, *I think I've been hanging around Kim way too long...hehe.*

After a long walk on the beach, Jazzman settles in the sand. She opens her journal and begins writing:

Dear Mom,

I MISS YOU! I still feel like you were taken from me too soon. I wish I asked you more questions. I wish I asked you about dad. I wish I had stayed in your hospital room as you took your last breath. I hope you understand that the doctor did not let me. I also wish we had more dialogue about your funeral arrangements. I know it's an unusual conversation to have, but how nice it would've been to know how you would have wanted things. What I wouldn't give for five more minutes with you.

Sometimes I wonder if you had something to do with protecting me in my job when Charles overlooked my hooking up with Afrique. It's such a big no-no in the music industry. I remember him giving me a look of disappointment, and that hurt me because I look up to him.

Mom, something is bothering me. Afrique wants me to move to Jamaica. Although, I love Jamaica and can find peace in paradise, I love my life in Miami and find peace here in my hometown. I'm having a hard time telling him no, I don't want to hurt his feelings.

Well, since I have a hard time saying no and want to please everyone close to me...I need something from you...I need YOUR STRENGTH! GIVE ME STRENGTH! 'Cause we know it's easy for me to say yes to please loved ones while hurting myself in the process.

Speaking of happy...as you know, I still believe that in order to have a successful career in the music industry I should be in FL, CA or NY. So, it's a...NO...to moving to Jamaica. And you already know I'm jealous that Tyson is moving to New York. JEALOUS & MAD! But as you used to tell me...this too shall pass.

You know mom, the reason why I never dated Tyson is his inability to commit to a long-term relationship. Tyson's lifestyle is so transparent to me. I see how he operates and I do not want to be just another woman in his life. I'm not criticizing him for his ways. The lifestyle we live makes it easy for us to have a good time and not commit. Or am I finding my own faults in other people. Am I scared to commit? I don't know how to answer that question. Or maybe I know, but I don't want to face it.

I don't know mom...I have so many questions. Do you think my obsession with Afrique has something to do with not having daddy in my life? To some degree do you think several of my decisions stem from his absence? I can sure use your words of wisdom right now. Please continue to protect me.

'TIL WE MEET AGAIN WITH A SUNSET

~ Love Jazzman ~

When Jazzman arrives back at the house she rushes in to the ringing phone. She picks it up just in time and short of breath. "Hello!"

"Hello, Jazzman. Is everything okay?"

Jazzman tries to catch her breath. "Hey, Jackie, yes. I just got in and thought you were Afrique calling."

Jackie still sounds worried, "Is everything okay with Afrique?"

Jazzman is wondering what the sudden concern is all about and wonders if she has been reading the tabloids too, "Yes, do you need to talk to him?"

Jackie informs Jazzman, "Well, he was supposed to pick up Desmond at school today and I got a call from the school."

"Oh my goodness. I'm so sorry." Jazzman feels bad.

Jackie gets upset, "Were you supposed to pick him up?"

Jazzman feels stuck in the middle, "No, I just got a call from him earlier today that he is not coming into town this weekend. So I assumed he called you, too. I'm so sorry he didn't call you."

Jackie calms down, "It's not your fault, Jazzman. I just wish that he could be more responsible if he can't make it. I wish he would stop assuming that just because he has great people in his life that it's all good, when it's not. We have things that we plan, too, and... I'm sorry...I'm just venting. I will have to change my plans."

"Again, Jackie, I'm so sorry and I would take Desmond for you, but I have to work this weekend."

"Thank you, Jazz, I know you would, but I need to have a talk with Afrique. Have a nice weekend."

"Okay, have a nice weekend as well." Jazzman hangs up the phone upset, wondering, *what the heck was he thinking? Did he think my plans were not as important as his? Does he think I can read minds and think I would just be his built-in babysitter? How unfair of him and selfish. Stop, Jazz. Maybe he is so upset he forgot.*

Chapter 10

SPRINGFIELD, MA
Jazzman and Afrique

Jazzman arrives at Afrique's hotel hoping to get some alone time with him to hash out their differences before his performance that evening. The whole point of her arriving early is to pump him up before the show and make up afterwards. At the end of the day, no matter how mad she is with him, she always wants him to have an awesome performance.

She is about to turn right towards the elevators when she sees the bar several feet away calling her name, urging her to take a shot before heading up to Afrique's room. She hesitates, but for some strange reason she still feels the need for a shot of tequila. When she turns toward the bar she sees Afrique with Diamond, her hand is on his arm, and their backs are towards her. Jazzman knows she can play this one of two ways: confront them or wait at his room to see if he enters alone. She thinks it's best to patiently wait for him in the room. She turns toward the elevator, when she hears Diamond say, "Yuh nuh want it?"

Hearing Diamond say that makes her cringe. It's enough to set Jazzman off, *I'm gonna deal with this shit right now!*

She marches right to the bar stating, "No! He doesn't because what he needs is right here. So, if you don't mind, you can take your hands off my man."

Diamond grows flustered. She turns to Afrique and says in patois, "She already getting possessive and she not even married to you, huh Afrique? Are you sure that's the type of woman you want?" Diamond slowly takes her hand off Afrique and stares Jazzman in the face.

Jazzman smiles so that Diamond can't see how pissed off she really is. "If you were in my shoes and your man was at the bar with me, I don't think you would be as civil as I'm being with you right now." Jazzman turns to Afrique, "What's this? Are you drunk? You have to be to hang with the likes of this."

Diamond laughs and gives Jazzman a pathetic look. "My man wouldn't have to be at the bar with another woman, because I wouldn't be the type of girlfriend to be all over other men that I work with." Diamond gets up from her seat to walk away, feeling like she's won the battle.

Jazzman knows that she is referring to Tyson. Jazzman and Diamond went to high school together. Diamond met with Jazzman and Tyson to strike a record deal years ago, but since Jazzman turned her down, she's had it out for Jazzman. She knew that Tyson was feeling her music, but at the time Jazzman was still calling the shots. So Diamond finally signed with a New York label when she moved to Brooklyn.

Jazzman is pissed that Afrique is exposing their business to Diamond. To control her emotions, she crosses her arms and responds, "Oh, is that what you say these days to get a man to cheat on his woman? What else do you say…'No one has to know but you and me?' I feel like we are back in high school, Davilla Grant."

Davilla is Diamond's birth name that she has hated since a young age. The meaning of the word is someone that comes from a village. In her case, she does and Jamaicans consider it the country. While still a little girl in Jamaica, her uncle took her innocence away from her, and he would call her by her name every time he raped her. That's why she despises her birth name to this day. What gave her strength was her desire to be a star and change her stage name to Diamond. She always saw herself as a person with potential but at the time she lacked the final touches. As a teen she liked the phrase 'diamond in the rough' because diamonds standout. She loves the way it takes years for it's beauty to form and she loves its unique shine that comes from the way it's cut. With time, she knew having a more developed figure and growing some confidence, would help her shine just like a Diamond.

Jazzman sees Diamond's face turn beet red and knowing she got her upset she giggles to herself.

Before anything else can be said, Afrique gets up and drops a fifty at the bar. "Enough!"

"I'll talk to you later, Afrique." Diamond walks away.

"Lata!" He yells out so she could hear him. Afrique gives Jazzman a disappointed look. "I don't even know what to say to you."

"How about saying, 'It's nice to see you.' Or 'Thank you for traveling during your busy time at work to see me.' Or 'I'm sorry I couldn't make it to Miami to see you cause I was too upset to have a conversation with you.' Is that what you meant to say?"

Afrique is pissed off. "I would be lying if I said that."

"Wow. Now I don't know what to say."

Afrique tries to make light of what he just said. "I wasn't expecting you and I needed some time to think." Then he says sarcastically, "You should be able to understand that."

Jazzman turns to walk away. "Take all the time you need, but I'm not sure I'll be around when you are ready to talk."

When she says that, he assumes she is referring to her stay in Springfield. Instead she is referring to their relationship, since she feels betrayed.

Afrique calls out to her, but she doesn't respond. She heard him say that she misunderstood what Diamond stated. The moment felt like déjà vu. She has been through this with him before, with Jackie. He would tell her what he thought she wanted or needed to hear instead of being honest with her.

So, she walks away feeling like he is getting ready to sugar coat this situation in order to have his cake and eat it, too.

However, this time he is being honest and it hurts like hell. What Jazzman doesn't hear, what she doesn't allow him to explain, is that Diamond's comment was referring to their performance in Connecticut. When Diamond shouts:

"Connecticut yuh ready for me to check fi yuh? YUH NUH WANT IT? Connecticut, are you ready for Afrique?"

They were discussing how to change the dialogue in the performance and tease the audience a while longer.

Jazzman is hurt and walking away seems like the right thing to do before she says something she might regret later. She doesn't want to give him the satisfaction of seeing her tears, so she leaves not knowing she is misunderstanding the situation.

꙳

SPRINGFIELD, MA
Afrique and Diamond

While Jazzman is en route back to Miami, Afrique is in the fitness center working off the stress. He is upset that he is getting blamed for something he is not doing. He is starting to feel like being in a relationship is not all it's cracked up to be when trust is an issue. He loves Jazzman, but he needs his space right now. He thought he knew her, but now he finds himself questioning their relationship. He is starting to feel that if he is going to get blamed for something he might as well act on it. Not to mention, he already feels like he is sharing her with Tyson.

After his workout, he looks for Diamond to apologize for Jazzman's behavior. He did not want any bad blood between them since they have to go on stage practically every night to perform together. He knows their chemistry on stage is keeping them hot and increasing their cash flow. So, Afrique will not let anything or anyone get in the way of his money or his success.

He didn't have to look far. He found her in her hotel room. She is at her balcony, getting some fresh air and that is where they sit to talk. She is still upset and he helps her calm down. He senses she needs a friend.

He allows her to rest her head on his chest as they sit there in silence for a few minutes.

Then Afrique finally asks, "Yuh good?"

"Yah mon. Me no know why yuh girl has it out for me. Me nuh do nothin' to her, yuh know." Diamond stays resting her head on his chest.

"She's had it rough. Don't take it personal."

Diamond sucks her teeth, "That's no excuse. We all been through tings. It no give her da right to treat me like shit or assume tings without getting to know me." Diamond says this knowing that Jazzman has made it that much easier for her to make moves on Afrique.

"Yuh right, but understand she's over there and I'm over here. She worries and I can't blame her." Afrique rubs Diamonds shoulder.

Diamond asks, "And I understand, but she needs to trust you. She does trust you, right?"

Afrique answers, "Ya mon, in her own way. She works in da industry, she understands the way tings work pon da road. So she worries, respectfully so."

Diamond pulls away so her eyes connect with his, "I understand. However, it still nuh give her da right to treat me dat way."

He allows his eyes to stay connected with hers when he asks with concern, "What happen to yuh Diamond? What's your story?"

The mood changes and she is not sure what he knows. She turns away and responds, "You dare ask. It doesn't matter."

"It does to me." He pulls her attention back to him, "Talk to me, tell me. Let me be here for you."

She shakes her head from side to side, "I can't." Her eyes are full of pain.

He pulls her close, "Trust me!"

Diamond asks with fear in her eyes, "Why should I?"

"Because in me you will have a friend for life."

She replies, "There is no guarantee in friendships."

He shakes his head in agreement, "True! But sometimes yuh have to take dat leap of faith."

She sighs deeply and is emotional as she says, "I'm dat girl dat grew up in Jamaica, feeling alone and feeling like no one understood me. Always asking 'why me?' I had that 'uncle', a friend of the family dat took advantage of me, an innocent little girl. Dat little girl wanted to scream and tell someone, but she was told dat telling will result in never seeing her family again. So, I remain silent because I knew I did not want to lose my family and live with him taking advantage of me everyday." Diamond reaches to wipe away her tears, but Afrique reaches them first and he wipes them for her.

"I'm sorry dat you had to live through dat. It must have been hard. I can't begin to understand your pain." Afrique gently laces his hand with hers giving her a firm hold letting her know that he is there for her.

Diamond tries to hide her pain through a half smile, "Thank you for caring."

He notices the pain and says, "Thank you for trusting in me. Remember, you don't have to hide your pain with me. We are friends now! You can show me and tell me what you are really feeling."

Diamond feels comfortable, so she continues, "Yuh know, there is a poem I wrote when I finally realized what was going on…knowing it was wrong…I've memorized it."

He asks, "Can you share it with me?"

Diamond takes a deep breath and exhales saying, "Here it goes…

When I look outside to see the light
My vision is blocked with the terror inside
Screaming with fear
Yelling for hope

That some day soon I would see day and not the night
My heart has been stabbed with so many lies
But I stood strong and fought back hard
I have dreamed so many dreams
I have cried so many nights
And never let the outside world
Come in my closed door
For they were the ones who put me there
Without knowing the damage they have done
In time they will see
Who has mended a bleeding heart
I will remain the strong one
And come out on top
Because my journey has been through a nightmare
That has not taken my life..."

She wipes away her tears and smiles asking, "Now do you regret wanting to know about me?"

Afrique half smiles and says, "Not at all. Thank you for sharing that with me. It's harsh, but I'm proud of you for overcoming a difficult time in your life. Be proud that your trials have made you a strong woman. And you picked the perfect name, Diamond. You are beautiful, unique and rare. Understand that your experience made you stronger. You've overcome a major obstacle in your life to make it in this business. Always be proud of your accomplishments. Most people would let that trauma defeat them. It would be their reason for why they can't succeed but you turned your experience into a positive. Always be proud. You still have a lot to accomplish and I can't wait to see what becomes of you, Diamond. With every song, every CD, every stage you set foot on and through your career milestones you will shine, like a unique Diamond." Afrique takes a strand of her hair and sweeps it behind her ear to get a glimpse of her flawless face. "You are beautiful. Always know and feel your beauty. You are perfect the way you are."

"Thank you! Thank you for your kind words. It means a lot to me." She places a gentle kiss on his cheek. This moment is special to her, sharing a part of herself that she does not share often. It feels innocent and she wants to explore more moments like this with him. "Well, I have a show to get ready for tonight and so do you."

"Yes, we do. This was nice, thank you." Afrique reciprocates the kiss placing it on her forehead. Yet, he's feeling somewhat guilty that he has not resolved his matters with Jazzman. He can't believe that he did not go after her when she walked away and asks himself, *what was I thinking?*

MIAMI, FL
Jazzman

Jazzman gets on the plane to head back to Miami. Since Afrique said he needs space it is up to him to make the effort to talk. She thought about going back and talking through their disagreement. However, she did not have the energy to try and convince him that it's imperative they hash out or compromise on their differences. She is worried that she will end up with a "get back guy", another guy to help her get over her madness, feel good for the moment and feel like crap later for doing it. She feels the urge coming on, not knowing if Afrique is playing her with Diamond and not wanting this type of bad situation repeating in her life. She has been here before with her ex-boyfriend, Mike, and has not been the same since. It took her a long time to get over Mike and to heal from that relationship.

She feels a mean streak coming on, 'screw him before he screws you'. Subconsciously this is her attitude when it comes to men. She reacts when she feels a guy might hurt her and she will deliberately hurt him before he can cause her pain. Little does Afrique know, his clock is ticking.

During her time on the plane, Jazzman takes time to think of the pros and cons. She is still uncertain as to what to do with Afrique. She feels a headache coming on, so she switches gears to think back to her first directing gig on Bimma's music video. The time on the video set brought her a dose of new confidence. She remembers her emotions going from nervous jitters to exploding excitement in overseeing the project transform from a script and into motion. The moment when she called, "It's a wrap", was a rush, feeling accomplished at finishing her first music video. The joy that filled her heart was the most rewarding. It was a pivotal moment in her career, reaching another goal. She knows that her success helps her to overcome stressful moments in her life and she wants to move forward in seeking her dreams. Jazzman feels something in her life has to change, but she is unclear of the best solution. She wants to continue on her journey of following her dreams and she is not sure if Afrique will be part of that journey.

Jazzman thinks to herself, *I'm pissed at what happened with him, but my airplane ticket was money well spent. At least, that's how I have to look at it so I don't get even more pissed off. I'm not wasting my energy on this crap. My time sitting on this plane has helped me to realize that I'm most complete when seeking my dreams. I also know that I'm not a limelight girl. I love being behind the scenes making magic for all to see and feel. This moment has helped me to see that no matter where things end up with Afrique, I need to get my shit together. I need to get my damn thoughts in order to protect...my...self...worth and the career that I have worked so hard to build. With that said, please Lord, give me strength. I need it! I also need more therapy.*

As the airplane lands, Jazzman convinces herself that she has life figured out and maybe she no longer needs therapy to keep peace at home. She thinks, *I don't want to hear Afrique's mouth every time I go to therapy. So, my therapy will work itself out through prayer, friendships and staying focused on my career. I have neglected my career by putting Afrique's needs before mine. Ever since he proposed to me, I thought putting him first was the right thing to do in order to form our family. Now, I have to refocus and decide what's best for me. Lord, help me.*

By the time she drives home she is convinced of her next step. She grabs water from the refrigerator but when she sits down, she begins to doubt herself again. One thing is for sure, she can't imagine her life without Afrique. Thinking about their times together, she realizes she has found the best partner and the best intimacy in her life.

She grows mad at herself for not hearing Afrique out after she exploded in Springfield. Maybe there was an explanation for what was going on. She fantasizes of how the night would have played out if she had taken a moment to listen to him:

> She shuts him up mid-way through their argument exposing a hint of flesh. The gesture excites him giving him the message that if he plays nice he will receive pleasure and give her some pain. They make their way to his suite.
>
> She throws him on the bed and ties his hands. The pleasure begins, as she places licks upon his skin, her touch arouses him. With each kiss her love is injected into his body and his reaction to those kisses excites her to please him through the night.
>
> She allows him to return the favor as he ties her hands for his own delight. He has his way with her body, exploring with his tongue. His touch of love awakens her senses as she moans in satisfaction. He reminds her how beautiful she is as his fingertips trace her figure, bringing her body to life. His stroke causes her to crave what he has to offer, and his taunting ways makes her feel out of control, begging for more. His quest to please her takes her body to the climax she desires.

BANG

Jazzman snaps back to reality when her bottled water falls to the floor. She is feeling aroused and a little depressed as her heart races from imagining what she is not able to have at the moment. It nearly drives her insane. She paces around the house unsure of what to do with the free time on her hands. She tries to take a nap, but her thoughts are out of control. She walks over to the sofa and listens to music, but each song reminds her of Afrique.

She is tired of her thoughts, tired of thinking about therapy and Afrique, realizing she needs a break from it all. She thinks for a moment about what else she could be doing at this time. So, rather than waste a perfectly good day daydreaming or sitting at home feeling sorry for herself, she contacts Oriba.

When Oriba arrives at Jazzman's house they get right down to business with music, food and Merlot. It's a perfect night to brainstorm on a concept for his first music video.

After a couple of hours of strategizing on song choice, they narrow it down to two songs. Another glass of wine, gives them the winner, "How Does It Feel". They both agreed the beat will bring DJs to keep the song on constant rotation, especially at the clubs. The only concern they have is topping a masterpiece. However, Jazzman reassures Oriba that her business skills will keep him hot.

Now that they have the song, they get to work on a concept for the music video. Jazzman uses her own trials and tribulations with Afrique and Diamond to create a music video concept. It's time well spent and for Jazzman it is allowing her to release her tension. In a weird way it helps her deal with her situation. It also gives her insight as well as some strength for what she will have to go through in order to resolve those problems.

The time with Oriba reinforces for her that as long as she has a job she loves, it will help her get through the darkest moments in her life. So with that in mind, she begins to work on Oriba's CD release. She prays the time will allow her to find the answers she needs on how to handle her situation with Afrique.

Chapter 11

BOSTON, MA
Afrique and Diamond

After another great show, Afrique and Diamond are full of energy. Their entire crew is feeling the same way so they continue their night at Club Roxi. They had heard this club is the place to be with DJ Lox on the turntables. He is well known and anywhere he is playing, people are bound to have a good night.

Tonight is no different – reggae night and it's the right music to celebrate the success of their sold out concert. The VIP room is reserved for Afrique, Diamond, their crew, press, music industry folks and a few local celebrities. The room is on the second floor overlooking the dance floor through a glass window. The all white furniture and florescent blue lights make the room sleek and inviting.

Bottles are 'poppin', glasses are filled with champagne, wine, mixed drinks, hard liquor and shots. Afrique is feeling good and so is Diamond. Their energy is rubbing off on everyone around them. Afrique and Diamond first get down to business, giving the press what they want, interviews, followed by several side bar conversations with music industry folks. By the time they are done with the press, what had been fifty people in the room, dwindled down to twenty people ready to really party.

As the night went on, more dancing, drinking and laughing filled the room. The crowd is feeling good and bodies are releasing tension to the beat of the music. Every thump, every boom, lets out an arousal, bringing the people to put their hands up in the air in agreement with the lyrics. Over the next hour, the number of people in the room decreased to just a handful. However, when it's announced that the dance contest will begin in fifteen minutes, even the remaining party people in the VIP room make their way to the dance floor.

By this time, it is obvious that Afrique and Diamond are getting cozy on the sofa. When the song, "Romping Shop" by Vybz Kartel featuring Spice, begins to blast on the speakers, Diamond releases her energy by dancing for Afrique. Her offering comes as a lap dance that leaves him no choice but to stay in position and enjoy the ride. At first, Afrique half-heartedly tries to refuse due to his commitment to Jazzman.

As Afrique resists he says, "No, I can't do this."

Diamond reassures him, "No one will know."

He tells himself, *you will regret this later.*

However, as Afrique's thoughts weigh on him, so does Diamond with her ass swaying in front of his eyes, as tempting as delicious fruit hanging from a tree. His thoughts taunt him and he plays in his head what Diamond told him at the hotel room, *'She is not all that innocent yuh know. You keep tinkin yuh have da golden prize. Let me guess, is it Oriba the one that wants her? Aren't they in the studio working on an album? Or is it her partner...what's his name... Tyson. He wants her! Those two belong together, just like you and I belong together.'*

His frustration with Jazzman gets the best of him. It's enough to put him over the edge, allowing Diamond to do her thing. It's an Adam and Eve moment ripe with temptation. He condones her moves by allowing his hands to caress parts of her body as she rubs against him, giving his body the attention it needs.

Their dance creates an air of intimacy that leads the bartender and waitress to feel uncomfortable and quietly exit the room.

The bartender turns to the waitress, "I thought he was seeing someone?"

The waitress replies, "Maybe they broke up. You know industry relationships, they don't last long."

The bartender agrees, "True."

Neither Diamond nor Afrique even notice their departure. In a zone, all they see is each other and the intensity of their desire grows with each beat and each successive touch. Their animal instincts are in top gear.

When Diamond whispers in his ear, he pulls her back by her hair, she smiles in excitement and he pulls her hair back even further. As her neck is exposed, he attacks it like a vampire wanting to suck blood. She screams in excitement asking for more, guiding his lips to her breasts to give them the same intense satisfaction. He obeys and gives her what she wants as she pushes his head against her body.

Then, Diamond pulls Afrique up and pushes him against the wall so she can salute his midsection with her lips. When the sensation brings Afrique to the edge, he pulls her off firmly placing her on the table facing the window that overlooks the dance floor. He nibbles at her back, section by section. As he approaches her ass he rips her panties off and drives his erect penis into her much needed body. As their bodies move toward each other, in and out, in and out, Afrique enjoys the view, doggy-style. He is pulling her towards him and she is pushing her ass into him, in synch they are satisfying each other.

She, too, is enjoying every moment and she is visible to the dancers on the dance floor, to the few that left the room who peek up in curiosity. Although they could not see Afrique many know who is with her, and from her expression it is obvious what is taking place. Two of the people look at each other wondering the same thing, wondering why Afrique is carrying on that way. They were under the impression that he was seeing someone. They watch as her hair is pulled back even further exposing more of her pleased facial expression.

Her body is completely exposed to the dry air of the night, yet completely wet on the inside from Afrique's touch. She moans for more, "Harder!"

He obeys giving her what they both need. There is no pausing their play, not even an officer flashing his badge could stop their action. They were past the point of disturbing the peace; they were animals in heat and could not be tamed.

Diamond has had one mission with Afrique and she conquers her quest tonight. She started off as a pleasure-seeker. Tonight she permitted her territory to be marked, allowing Afrique to put his stake in the ground. By the end of the night, their bodies discover several rounds of unfamiliar territory.

MIAMI, FL
Jazzman

Jazzman opens the door to exit the building and sees sunlight after a twenty-four hour shift at the studio with Oriba. From the moment she opens the door, she is hit with self-discovery that she will begin living her life making sure that she is fulfilling her own happiness.

However, her moment of self-empowerment is short lived when she stops at the bodega for *café con leche*. As she waits for the coffee, the newspaper stand catches her eye. A couple of tabloid newspapers have Afrique and Diamond on the cover. She takes a moment to scan through one of the more reputable sources and the core of her being is aching as she reads the article. It has a picture of the two of them in a very intimate stance and the article is referring to them as a couple.

After paying for her coffee and the magazine she walks to her car. The pain makes it hard for her to breathe. When she turns on the ignition, the radio stations are also talking about them.

Jazzman drives all the way to work not wanting to set foot in the office. Her stomach is twisted up in a knot. She weathers the storm by going any way, but all eyes are on her from the moment she sets foot in the building. She feels exposed, completely uncomfortable and not knowing what to say if someone asks her about Afrique. She goes into her office and closes the door behind her. She remains there the whole day in a daze, from time to time trying to get work done. She had scheduled another trip to surprise Afrique, but with today's news she tells her assistant to cancel it.

When Tyson sees her during a department meeting, even he doesn't say a word to her other than a work related comment or two. Jazzman notices that the few good friends she has at the office are looking at her funny. She can't blame them, understanding they are probably unsure of how to approach her about the situation. She wants to talk to someone to release her feelings, however she is too upset to say a word.

She also convinces herself there is a flip side of what she read, telling herself that she can't be sure of the validity of the source. All she knows is she left Springfield feeling that things between them will never be the same.

As far as Jazzman is concerned, if she confronts Afrique and he were to say there is nothing going on, she won't believe him. For Jazzman, a picture is worth a thousand words and by the looks of it there is something there. There is something between them and she doesn't want to compete for someone's love. She can only take so much of the women that are continuously throwing themselves at him for a piece of fame and not caring who they hurt in the process.

Her questions about Afrique possibly cheating bring to mind the time when they first met and his dishonesty about his situation. Since he was not truthful with her it caused her to form her own opinion. It caused her to feel like she was the mistress, and it was an uncomfortable feeling. Similar feelings surface now and it feels like déjà vu, all over again. The need to put her guard up is back.

She thinks, *just when I talk myself into being cured and not needing therapy, Lord, you find interesting ways of setting me straight and letting me know what I really need. I'm so pissed. I need to vent. I will call my therapist for another appointment. I don't know how much more I can take. I don't want to cry. Give me strength. I need it.*

Chapter 12

MIAMI, FL
Tyson & Friends

~ FAST FORWARD ~
Farewell Cookout:
After Tyson's New Orleans Trip With Jazz

[R&B Music Playing]

It's another hot day in Miami, the smell of barbeque mixed with Mr. Banks's special seasoning fills the air. All invited show up in support of a man who has worked hard and will be missed when he leaves to New York.

Tyson's whole life has been a testament to his character. Growing up when he was tempted to stray, his dad was there to let him fall, but always two steps behind to help him back up. His dad taught him to be a humble man, and to have the patience to wait for what is rightfully his. Today is a celebration of another one of his victories of lessons learned.

People arrive while Tyson and his dad are setting up and Mrs. Banks is in the house preparing side dishes. The appetizers are already out on the tables for people to munch on while they socialize, until the main festivities begin. The DJ is mixing on the turntables switching between classic R&B, contemporary R&B and Hip Hop.

After some time of chatting with guests, Tyson goes inside to check on his mom. Mrs. Banks indicates that a couple of the side dishes are ready to be brought outside. When he grabs the macaroni and cheese dish and the tuna salad he looks up at the clock. An hour has passed since the guests started to arrive.

Mrs. Bank states, "Don't worry she will show up."

Tyson responds, "I don't know, ma. I don't think so, not this time."

Mrs. Banks smiles. She has had this conversation with her son many times before. "Son, who is your mother?"

Tyson smiles, "You, Ma!"

She asks, "And have I ever been wrong?"

"No," says a voice from the doorway, and Jazzman walks in, almost as if on cue.

Mrs. Banks smiles, "Hello!"

Jazzman smiles back, "Hello!"

There is unusual awkwardness between Jazzman and Tyson and Mrs. Banks senses it. Tyson nods what's up. "You're late, but I'm glad you could make it. Well, I have to bring these outside. See you in a few?"

"Sure." Jazzman replies, but sounding a bit distant. Despite the situation she knows she wouldn't have forgiven herself if she were a no-show.

Tyson excuses himself and Jazzman sits down looking like she just lost her best friend. "Hello Ma. Do you need help with anything?"

Mrs. Banks takes a good look at Jazzman. "Now baby girl, as long as you've been coming here you should know by now I've got all this under control."

"Please, I need to be doing something...I mean I need to help with something." Jazzman can't seem to shake the blues.

Recognizing that Jazzman needs to be busy, she replies, "You can peel the potatoes for the potato salad."

"Thank you!" Jazzman, being very familiar with the Banks kitchen grabs a potato peeler from the silverware drawer, a bowl from the cabinet and sits down to begin peeling the potatoes.

Mrs. Banks knows of Jazzman's relationship with Afrique, but at this moment she is concerned with the sadness in Jazzman's eyes. Only once before has she seen Jazzman look so lost and that was when her mom passed. Other than that, she always noticed her eyes light up the room especially right after glancing at Tyson and exchanging a hello. Their eyes tell a story when they are around one another. Today was extremely different.

Mrs. Banks inquires, "You're here, but your mind seems far away. You look like you have a lot on your mind."

Jazzman shakes her head, "My apologies, Mrs. Banks. I do have a lot on my mind." Wanting to change the subject Jazzman says, "Where are my manners? I don't think I even asked how you are doing today."

"I'm okay, baby girl. Obviously, not great with my baby boy going to New York, but knowing he is pursuing his dreams gives me comfort and joy. Question is 'how are you doing'?"

Jazzman stops peeling the potatoes, "I'm just okay, too. A lot on my mind."

"I see. That look tells me it has something to do with a man." Mrs. Banks looks at her, waiting for a truthful response.

Jazzman can't hold it any longer so she asks, "Mrs. Banks, how did you know Mr. Banks was the one? How do you know when one guy is the right one for you? When do you know to follow your heart?"

"Those are loaded questions, my dear. It's something a lot of people question time and time again. First, let me start off by saying only you will know the right one for you and you will know. You know there are some people that search their whole life for love. Some people close their hearts to love when a past relationship has hurt them deeply. There are some that love from the heart and some that love with the brain. Those are usually the ones that marry for money. Some people are afraid to take a leap of faith with a friend, afraid to take that friendship to another level. Some people confuse love with hurt, assuming it isn't true love if it doesn't hurt sometimes. But… always remember that love is patient and kind. The right man will be your friend and your lover. He will love you just the way you are and will accept your imperfections as part of the whole package that is you."

"I see." It was not quite the response she was looking for and left her still wondering about love. Jazzman picks up another potato to peel.

As if Ms. Banks could read her mind she states, "There is no easy answer for this one, baby girl. Sometimes you just have to follow your heart. And there will be one man you can't live without. I can tell you my experience. You know, Mr. Banks was not the only man trying to woo me when we got together. There was a man named Clark; he was the kind of guy I couldn't bring home to my mama. But darling, it was easy falling for his smooth lines and believing everything he told me. Luckily, I had good friends around me to help me see clearly. My momma always told me…a man needs to be crazier about you than you are about him. You see, when I was first getting to know Tyson's daddy I could tell he was the type of man to stay by my side if I got sick. I knew he would not take advantage of situations to seek other women. When I was getting to know Mr. Banks there was no drama. It just clicked. Our relationship developed with ease. Sometimes, Jazzman, it's all about timing. That person can be right in front of you, but if it isn't the right time, it won't work. You usually do know when he ISN'T the right one. You get plenty of signs along the way. You might not want to see them, but you feel them. And although you may know right away that a man is the one, you should never marry anyone until you've spent at least a year getting to know them. That way you get to see how they react and treat you through many different events. You will know in time…God will let you know, if you listen with your heart and your mind." Mrs. Banks gives Jazzman a much needed hug. "Now enough of this talk. This is a party and you need to get outside and mingle with the rest of the folks."

"Thank you." Jazzman hugs Mrs. Banks.

She goes outside feeling somewhat out of place, like she has a red bulls eye on her forehead. She wonders how many people at the party read the tabloids and are making speculations about her relationship with Afrique. It does not feel good.

As Jazzman is wondering about that, everyone at the party is sensing something might be wrong between her and Tyson. Most of them think it's due to two friends getting ready to live apart. Even Kim and Jordan, their closest friends, are wondering what the deal is between them. Jackie asks Jordan if he knows if anything has happened between Jazz and Tyson in New Orleans, but he doesn't have any information to share.

As Jazzman makes her way through the crowd, she turns her attention toward Jordan, Jackie and Desmond. Jazzman asks if she can entertain Desmond to give Jackie and Jordan some adult time. They appreciate Jazzman's kindness, but it's also Jazzman's way of avoiding feeling out of place. After an hour of quality time with Jordan, Jackie asks him to take over watching Desmond, so she can have a personal conversation with Jazzman. When Jackie asks her if they could talk, Jazzman's stomach develops a knot, unsure of the topic. It has always bothered Jazzman that Jackie is so close to her situation. Jazzman has always felt uncomfortable with the fact that Jackie could know more about her life than she would care for her to know, being close to both Afrique and Tyson.

As they take a seat on two lawn chairs away from the crowd, Jackie says, "Thank you for watching Desmond so Jordan and I could have some adult time."

Jazzman smiles, "You don't have to thank me. I enjoy spending time with him."

Jackie begins to probe. "I know. It shows and he enjoys spending time with you. However, don't take this the wrong way, but that concerns me. It's only been you spending time with Desmond. Afrique has not been making time for him. Is everything okay?"

"Well, you know he's been busy with the tour. So, it's been difficult for him to make the time that he would like to make for Desmond." Jazzman, nervously takes a sip of her drink.

"Well again, please don't take this the wrong way, but until he can make more of a commitment to spend time with his son, I will cut back on his visits." Jackie takes a sip of her drink as well.

"I understand. Have you talked to him?" Jazzman wonders.

"I've already brought it to his attention, but I want to let you know woman to woman. I don't want you to take it personal because I appreciate you being there for Desmond. This is one of the reasons why things did not work between us; he wasn't there for Desmond. He thought he was doing his part just by working hard and providing for us, but 'things' do not take the place of one's time." Jackie rubs Jazzman shoulder. "You know, I know it is none of my business, but I've been in your shoes. It gets lonely waiting for a man on the road."

"Jackie, please don't take this the wrong way, but you're right, it's none of your business." Jazzman tries to hide her emotions and gets up abruptly to signal that the conversation is over.

"I'm sorry if I've overstepped my boundaries. Enjoy the rest of the day." Jackie gets up and quickly walks back towards Jordan and Desmond.

Jazzman immediately feels bad, knowing Jackie wasn't the cause of her frustration. It was Afrique's behavior and her insecurities that led her to snap at Jackie. "Jackie, wait...I...I appreciate you taking the time to let me know what's going on."

Jackie gives her a half smile and before walking away she adds, "Jazz, all I know is that with Afrique on tour things aren't as easy for any of us. I know I took you off guard with this conversation, so maybe we can revisit this later this week. If you want to talk, that is."

"I think I'd like that, thanks." Jazzman gives Jackie a half smile.

Jackie walks off and walks towards the two men in her life.

Once again, Jazzman is feeling so alone. Afrique is not here with her, Kim has Rick and her best friend is leaving soon. She feels like she is a bit lost in both her love life and her career. She has heard that sometimes these challenges need to happen in order to help propel people into reaching their true potential. She's often heard about the importance of really finding one self before moving on to face the larger obstacles in life and how small steps develop ones wisdom to succeed. Nonetheless, this is not feeling good to her. She knows that going to therapy and releasing the feelings that are bottled up inside is helping her heal and find some inner peace. But right now she is feeling extremely alone and unsure of herself.

"You look like you can use a friend." Tyson is standing behind her. When Jazzman turns around to face him, he raises her chin up in order for their eyes to connect. "Jazz, you don't need to worry about our friendship. I think you and I both know what we share will last forever, despite the distance."

Her eyes water immediately. "How can you be so sure? I think we both know that things might never be the same between us."

"Our friendship has endured some hard times. I know we can manage through this. Some distance might even help us. Besides, New York is not the end of the world you know." He looks into her eyes forcing her to be truthful. "What are you thinking?"

"I'm scared of losing you. I'm scared and I don't know what to do with these feelings. I'm going to miss you, my friend." She wipes away her tears.

He knows what she means and manages to say, "I know the feeling." He says this knowing a part of him wants the distance between them. Yet the other part of him feels strongly that this is not what he needs. He only wishes that she could come to her senses with her choices in life.

"I have to get going, but I want you to know that I will miss you so much." Jazzman reaches out to give him a hug. They hug so tight that it's hard to let go and she asks, "Will we see each other before you leave?"

He is enjoying her hug saying, "I'm not sure. I'm almost through packing, but still have several other things to get done. I'll try to call you before I take off. Otherwise I'll call you as soon as I get settled in

New York. I'll expect a visit, too, you know. I mean New York is only a short flight away."

She lets go. "Would you tell your mom and dad I said bye?"

He smiles, "Will do."

She continues, "—I'm not up to that added emotional stress right now."

"They'll understand."

"I'll check up on them when you're gone."

He smiles again, "That's very kind of you to do. I appreciate it." He thinks back to his time with her in New Orleans. He knows she needs time alone and he understands as he needs the same. He watches her walk away as if it were the last time he would see her. He almost goes after her, tempted to tell her more about his own feelings, but he holds back knowing he needs to let things play themselves out in their own way and in their own time - something else he learned from his dad.

Meanwhile, inside the house, Mr. Banks notices Jazzman leaving and he turns to Mrs. Banks, "Jazzman is leaving without saying good-bye. That's not like her."

Mrs. Banks informs him, "She has a lot on her mind."

Mr. Banks responds, "I can see that. I just hope she is okay. Tyson said everything went well in New Orleans. I hope it did. Tyson didn't say much, but when I gave her a hug today, it felt weird. I hope I made the right decision helping Tyson prepare for that trip."

Mrs. Banks reassures him, "Well, we can talk to him tonight after everyone leaves."

After everyone leaves, Tyson takes a moment to enjoy the anticipation of his future. It feels too good to be true. There are times when doubt fills his head about moving. Yet, he pushes through those thoughts, reminding himself the only way to get to the next level is by walking through the open door when opportunity presents itself. A part of him feels bad for Jazzman, knowing she should be the one going to New York. However, he also knows that he, too has worked hard for this, and everything happens for a reason. So, he will gladly take his position and make the move to New York City where bright lights shine on dreams bursting to come alive.

He stops a moment and his mind turns to thoughts of Jazzman and his time with her in New Orleans.

At the same moment, Jazzman is in her car driving, also thinking about their 'special' week in New Orleans.

Chapter 13

NEW ORLEANS, LA

Jazzman and Tyson

~ REWIND ~
New Orleans:
A Week Before Tyson's Farewell Cookout

[Jazz Music Playing]

Tyson and Jazzman have been enjoying the New Orleans Jazz Festival for the last two days. This event attracts so many people and for Jazzman it brings out mixed emotions. Her dad, a jazz musician, gave her the name 'Jazz-man' when he got back home from this festival many years ago. So, she has yearned to attend this festival for over twenty years. Up until now she had held back from going, somehow feeling it wouldn't be 'right' out of respect for her mother. When her dad would arrive home from tour or overnight gigs, sometimes he would accuse Jazzman's mother of cheating. She wonders if this was due to his insecurities and infidelities. The accusations started off subtly, but then slowly grew from small name-calling into arguments. Then, when verbal abuse wasn't enough to make his point, physical abuse took over. Eventually, Jazzman's mom took hold of the situation for the sake of her daughter and ended things before his next trip to New Orleans. He had said good-bye to her and that was it. She never heard from her father again.

Now that she is at Jazz Fest, she feels disloyal to her mom's memory. She has to keep checking herself and reminding herself that, "it is okay to have fun in New Orleans." So, she does just that, by taking a deep breath and focusing on work.

Scouting talent in the park is a challenge in itself and the hot sun beating down on Tyson and Jazzman is only aggravating the situation. They take turns applying sunscreen on their arms and face, and they assist one another, rubbing it on each other's back.

As Tyson rubs her back he can't help but to ask, "Do you need lotion anywhere else 'cause you know I wouldn't mind waxing that ass."

Jazzman playfully pushes him, "You wish! You know what, you are so lucky I'm in a good mood and that I know you."

The music is soothing. The afternoon heat leads them to find a spot in the shade. Jazzman pulls out a towel from her backpack, placing it on the ground for them to share. Tyson sits beside her, moving a strand of hair away from her face.

She smiles and says, "Thank you."

He smiles back, "No problem. What are good friends for?"

"You had to get the 'good' in there, mark your territory, my friend."

Tyson still smiling, "A brother's gotta do, what a brother's gotta do. I'm going to be away for a while, so I have to make sure you forget me NOT. Not to mention I'm going to miss you."

"YOU? I'm going to miss you like crazy. How am I supposed to get by without you at the office and on a personal level? This is not cool, Tyse." Jazzman only calls him 'Tyse' when it's real serious.

"I know it's going to feel strange. I'm gonna have to find another momma at my new office." Tyson looks to see her reaction.

Her facial expression exposes shock with a hint of jealousy, the reaction he is hoping for, and she says, "You wouldn't!"

Tyson smiles revealing his perfect white teeth, "I got to. I'm a man! A man has needs and if I can't have you, I'm gonna find someone else to roll with me. Who knows maybe I'll find true love in the big apple. I'm saying if Kim found it, my chances are looking promising."

When it's put so bluntly, Jazzman realizes the thought terrifies her, even though she's not sure why. She replies casually, "There are a lot of beautiful women in New York. I wouldn't be surprised if one sinks her teeth into you. Are you sure Charles doesn't need me there with you?" Jazzman inquires.

She watches as Tyson's look changes to one of sadness, knowing inside she feels the same way. He does not want to go down this road with her again. "Hey, I've been wanting to ask you something, but not sure when the right time would be, so I'm just going to ask. Have you thought about looking for your dad? I know you were kind of upset when he left flowers at your mom's grave, but I thought maybe now with your momz gone you'd want to connect with him. I know we have talked about this prior to him leaving the flowers, but I'm just curious how you feel about it now."

Jazzman feels awkward. She was expecting him to joke, react or maybe even ask if she is making the right decision with Afrique. "I see we are changing the subject."

"Jazz, I give up on us being anything more than friends, at least for the time being. You are getting married and I respect your decision. You have to do what you think is best for you and I accept that. Don't worry. We are cool. I just want what's best for you."

"Understood! Sometimes I think...never mind...to answer your question about my dad, I have thought about it. My therapist asked me the same thing at my first visit. I wasn't sure then, but now that I'm here I think I do want to connect with my dad. You know being here with all these musicians and knowing this is or was, his venue, too, has confirmed it. Thanks!"

Tyson appears confused, "What did I do?"

Jazzman gazes into his eyes and for a moment the world stands still as he locks his eyes with hers. He gives her that look and she acknowledges it by saying, "You just know me. It's simple with you. You had this great idea of coming to New Orleans and somehow I find my answer here. You know since we've been here, when I see an older man I find myself wondering 'Is he my dad?' Then I see another man and say, 'Or maybe he's my dad'. It's crazy! I also worry about meeting him. I worry a lot about being thrilled to see him and forgetting about all the wrong he's done. Then I worry about not letting myself be happy, holding a grudge against him or not letting him into my life. I think about all the possibilities, but the one thing I don't know is who he is now, what is he like and how he will react if I do find him."

Tyson reassures her, "Jazz, I know he will be delighted to see you and proud of all your accomplishments. He's your dad and I know he must think of you."

"You think?" Jazzman feels a small hint of hope.

"I know so." Tyson places a gentle kiss on her cheek.

Jazzman whispers, "What was that for?"

"For the woman you are and your perseverance to live life despite the challenges you face. You don't let anything stop you! I'm proud of you."

"I love you." The words just slip out and although startled at how easy those words come to her lips, she's happy they did.

"Hmm…I love you, too, but watch what you say to me. There are plenty of hotels nearby we can check into and finish what we started in Jamaica." He winks seductively at her.

"Why? When we have the one we are already checked into." After saying that, she realizes she has put her foot in her mouth.

"Please girl, you think I would drive back to the other side of the Mississippi River and risk you changing your mind? I don't think so." He's happy he got that off his chest even though he knows a part of this conversation is in fun and the other part is a betrayal of truth lurking just beneath the surface in both of them.

Jazzman laughs, "I said it before and I'll say it again, you know me well."

"I'VE said it before and I'LL say IT again, Let's go! The hotel is that way." Tyson gives his fist to pound knuckles with Jazzman. They laugh and hug it out. Their bodies lock for what seems like forever, a part of them feeling scared and sad at knowing their time of seeing each other on a regular basis is coming to an end. Although the label has told Tyson six months to a year, they both know it can become a permanent move for him. This will be their second time away from each other for an extended period. The first time they were apart was miserable for both of them. The thought scares them knowing this move can either make their friendship stronger or it could tear them apart.

NEW ORLEANS, LA
Jazzman and Tyson

Tyson and Jazzman had a long day, so they decided to unwind at the hotel pool to discuss some of the entertainers they encountered thus far at Jazz Fest. After an hour of deliberation, they decide on three prospects to bring to Charles's attention. However, there were several entertainers that have yet to perform, which the locals have been talking about, so they are keeping an open mind.

Afterwards, they head up to Tyson's hotel room. Once inside the room, Tyson pours a drink for both of them and as he hands Jazz a glass he says, "This is a toast to my job in New York and to our friendship remaining strong."

Jazzman senses Tyson's nervousness and she quietly responds, "To New York and friendship."

After their toast, he says, "Please stay right here for a moment. I need to do something. Can you do that for me?"

She smiles, "Of course." She begins to wonder what has him on edge.

Seconds later, the music begins. Playing softly in the background, is a famous jazz song, "At Last". Jazzman's mind races back to the first time she heard this song. She was a little girl and her father played it for her time and time again. She remembers her dad telling her the song reminded him of the first time he gazed into her eyes at the hospital; he said he had found his dream. However, when the relationship went sour with her mother, he was gone and so was jazz music. Jazzman's mother banned it from their home.

Tyson plays the song for her knowing it will remind her of her dad.

She closes her eyes to stop the tears from escaping as the memories surface. Her concentration is broken as she feels Tyson's arms wrap around her waist. His touch sways her body into a dance and the feeling of security allows her to release the tears. "Thank you, I needed this."

In Tyson's arms, the song makes her feel loved. This is not the first time they have danced and she wonders if this is their last. She thinks back to the first time they went out salsa dancing. He was nervous but she reassured him he could dance, after all she was his teacher. Her dream-like state is interrupted when Tyson gently turns her away from him for a twirl. As she ends back to face him, they gaze at one another and are struck by the connection. Jazzman fights the feelings and looks away. Tyson gently caresses her cheek and brings her focus back to him. His gaze tells her to not fight the feeling, the power of their love. The desire to get a taste of the other's lips is present, but their bond to respect boundaries is even stronger.

Tyson tells himself again that she is not married yet and crossing the line at this moment is necessary to get Jazzman thinking. He knows that she takes her engagement seriously and she may take his kiss as an insult. So, he acts gentlemanly and lets the dance speak for him as he caresses her back allowing his hands to massage their way, all the way down to her lower back. He uses all his concentration to keep from going further, all the while thinking that Afrique is probably not keeping his hands to himself at the moment. Tyson's hands slowly move up her sides shocking the core of her being. Another warm gaze is shared, her deep brown eyes piercing into his soul. She kisses her index finger and seals it on his lips. He closes his eyes to let his mind wander to the possibilities of what he would do next. Before he opens his eyes, the song is over and Jazzman has pulled away.

He sees the sparkle in her eyes as she whispers, "I think it's time for me to go. Thank you for this dance. It was perfect."

Tyson places his hands on her sides and whispers in her ear, "You are perfect and it has been my pleasure. I can't help the way I feel. On that note I think I should go...wait this is my suite."

They both laugh.

He continues, "Before you leave I want you to think of something. Do you think, just maybe, that you are with Afrique because he reminds you of your dad? Maybe you are only marrying him because of your circumstances. Since your mom just passed and you two share that experience doesn't necessarily mean you two are good for one another. Just a thought, so please don't get mad. Goodnight."

She kisses him on the cheek. "Thank you. Goodnight." Needing some solo time, Jazzman goes for a stroll through town, and after an hour of walking she heads back to the hotel. She passes a club and hears salsa music playing. The music feels good to her so she goes inside.

As Jazzman walks in, she scopes the scene as she always does to get a sense of the club's energy. When she gets the confirmation she needs, she takes a seat at the bar. After ordering a Cosmopolitan and taking a sip, she looks around the club again. Her eyes are drawn to this one guy on the dance floor, who looks hot from the back. Before she knows it her glass is empty and she is ordering another Cosmo and a shot of Tequila.

However, it isn't until her second shot of Tequila, that the guy dancing becomes somewhat intriguing to her. He is a mystery man with a beret on. Even though there is a flock of women surrounding him, she manages a glimpse of his physique – he's wearing a muscle shirt and jeans. It's not exactly dancing attire but for some strange reason he is turning her on.

She tries to check him out, but the women are all over him, flaunting themselves and she begins to wonder if he is a celebrity. The scent in the air says he's a bad boy and she wonders, 'Can he dance'? She orders her third Cosmopolitan and gets her answer as he begins to dance salsa with two women.

The guy Jazzman is checking out is a confident man. It shows in the way he controls the women on the dance floor and it excites her even more as she takes another shot of Tequila.

She watches as he effortlessly spins one lady, while still engaging the other with his moves, giving them both constant attention. Both ladies are smiling and Jazzman is digging their energy as she takes a sip of her Cosmo. She wants to see the face that goes with the body. She wants to know who is turning her on, but there are too many spectators observing this show.

The lyrics to the song are very appropriate as the singer talks of loving women, loving their curves and their sex appeal. The song continues with lyrics of getting hold of a woman's body and kissing her all over and getting him hard. The way his body is moving, she wants to dance with him. As she continues to admire the view, she observes him taking another two women into his arms.

Her opportunity to dance with him is looking more promising, as a couple more women ask him to dance. This observation gives her some confirmation that he is not with a significant other. She takes another sip of her drink wanting to make sure that she is feeling just right before she strikes the courage to approach him to dance.

The women dancing with him bring his body to a slightly different direction. She gets a glimpse of his face, but as she takes another sip it turns into a gulp when she gets a good look at her mystery man. Her eyes connect with Tyson. She gets up, slightly off balance and tries to compose herself as she walks towards him. When she makes her way to the dance floor, it feels like everyone in the club has disappeared.

As if the DJ knows their story he changes the music to a ballad about friendship, a Spanish song that captures Tyson's feelings:

'I know you love him, but he will never look at
you the way I do. He will never see you the way I do

178

and he will never make you laugh the way I do. Stay, drink with me and tell me what you really feel. And I will show you with my lips how much I want you. Let my lips touch parts of your body that you never knew existed. I know this may sound crazy, but even he knows I'm the only one that can truly make you happy. So, why can't you see what everyone else knows? You belong with me. Come closer let me unzip your dress and caress your body. Let me guide you in the right direction, right here with me and let our souls unite for eternity.'

The song brings them close and once again, for the second time in one night, they were in each other's arms dancing. He needs her and he knows that she needs him. He knows she is going through a hard time with Afrique even though she is not sharing it with him. He read the tabloid comments about Afrique's 'relationship' with Diamond. Rumors have it that more is going on between them, but it isn't his place to tell her things based on rumors. He wants her to figure this one out on her own because when he meddles, he is the one who suffers. He is concerned about her, but he also knows her strength. So, for now all he wants is to show his friend a good time.

Tonight, Jazzman sees a side of Tyson that she has only heard of, the way the women go crazy over him. Seeing it tonight has opened her eyes to the man that has stood by her side for so long. In his arms she even wonders what their life would have been like if Mike was not in the picture when they first met. She wonders if they would have remained in each other's life this long. However, she also knows that everything happens for a reason and right now no questions, no thoughts, no Afrique…just living in the moment with the one man who has never let her down and is giving her what she needs.

⌒◦

NEW ORLEANS, LA
Jazzman and Tyson

"So, this is Bourbon Street." Jazzman stops and takes a picture of the street sign.

"This is it!" Tyson looks down Bourbon Street and is amazed at what he sees. He can only imagine what this street will look like tonight when they party it up.

The streets signature look is the French style balconies. It gives a rich warm feeling, inviting one to partake in the Mardi Gras atmosphere. Jazzman envisions herself in the past walking down Bourbon Street with a couture gown. She smiles wondering what type of men she would have been attracted to back in the day. Then she bounces back to the present to take in the timeless scenery.

Jazzman carefully takes a picture of the street. She takes her time, because she senses something is wrong with Tyson. She can't pinpoint what it is, but something is on his mind. The drive to Bourbon Street was a bit strange. She's not sure if it's something she said last night, or the fact that he is leaving soon.

They continue to walk down the street and she asks Tyson to take a picture of her. Right before taking it he shouts, "Say, 'Jazz music'."

Jazzman gives a confused look, "No, if I say that my lips will look crazy in the picture."

As she is talking Tyson snaps a picture and Jazzman playfully hits him on the shoulder. "Take another picture."

"Please—"

"Please!" Jazzman combs her hair with her fingers.

"Can I ask you something without you getting upset?" Tyson asks as he looks through the camera lens.

"Sure!"

Tyson smiles as he takes another picture of Jazzman. Then asks her again, "Why are you really with Afrique? Do you think you are with him in part just because he is a musician like your dad and maybe you're craving that missing part of your life?"

Jazzman tenses up. This time she feels like she needs to respond. She looks at him, then she manages to say, "Interesting perspective." She learned to say this, in her line of business when unsure of the issue at hand. "I still need more time before I answer that question." She thought she was strong enough to answer it, but she doesn't want to make this moment about Afrique, especially since more tabloids are popping up about him with Diamond.

Tyson knows he's got her attention, "It's just a thought...think about it. Maybe you should bring it up at your next therapy session."

"Perhaps I will. My turn...what's on your mind? You've been acting different all morning."

Tyson tries to cover his smile with his hand, "Nah, everything is cool. Why you ask?"

Jazzman mimics him and tries to cover her smile, "Cause I know you better than I know myself and if I had to guess I would say a surprise is up your sleeve. How am I doing?"

Jazzman looks at Tyson to see his reaction and it appears that underneath his dark chocolate complexion he is blushing. She smiles, "See, I knew it!"

Tyson turns around to brush away the 'busted' look on his face and turns back to Jazzman with all seriousness and says, "Actually, I do, but it's not what you think."

They arrive at an intimate courtyard and Tyson gestures for her to sit and he does the same.

Jazzman's happy spirits flush away. "You're confusing me, Tyse. What's up?"

"I did something, with my dad's help. And up until the other day I wasn't sure if you would be mad at me, but I know now in my heart that I did the right thing. At least, that is what I kept telling myself through the process."

Jazzman is intrigued, but puzzled. "What is it?"

Tyson answers nervously, "It's my going away present to you."

Jazzman is confused and wondering what the heck has him on the edge. "O-k-a-y—"

Still nervous, he gazes into her eyes almost pleading for forgiveness, "Please don't be mad at me. Please understand what I did came from a good place—" Tyson points at his heart, "—right here. I need you to be at peace with what you've had to deal with in life. At the end of the day your happiness is one of my priorities."

Jazzman is reacting to his nervousness and begins feeling the same way. Yet, she feels so touched by his message. "Please tell me what you did. I promise to understand and not be upset. You are my friend and have always been there for me. Please just tell me."

He takes a deep breath and lets out the moment of truth, "My dad used his detective connections and helped me...he helped me find your dad." He takes a moment and waits for her reaction.

Her tears start to flow and he pulls out a tissue to wipe them away. He continues, "I need you to understand I would not have done this if I knew you were totally against it, but some of our conversations led me to believe I was doing the right thing for you."

Jazzman is so emotional. "I don't know what to say. I know that you probably saved me from a bunch of grief. I don't know what to say."

He asks in a pleading tone, "Please say you are not mad?"

"Of course not. I can't believe you did this for me! Thank you! Where is he? When can I see him? I wonder what he looks like!"

Before she could ask another question, she hears the jazz song, "At Last" again and this time a funny feeling takes hold of her stomach - 'the clench', she calls it. She is sensing something familiar even in this unfamiliar place. She sees a man she recognizes appear from behind one of the trees. She stares at him as he gets closer. A medium build, average size male with strong African American features approaches her. However, she knows he is a hundred percent Puerto Rican. She calls out in a little girl voice, crying, "Papi, is that you?"

His eyes well up with tears, "It's me, baby girl, it's me." He reaches out his arms to hold her and he manages to cry out, "I'm so sorry, *mi hija*."

Before any other words are exchanged, Tyson says, "Jazzman, Tony, I'm going to leave you two to talk." They both thank Tyson, and Tyson turns to Jazzman and asks, "You good?"

She smiles at her dearest friend with sincerity written in her eyes she responds, "I'm good."

"Okay, we will talk later." Tyson turns to Tony, "Take care of my friend."

"I will." Tony shakes Tyson's hand before he walks away and thanks him one more time.

Tony turns his attention back to Jazzman and continues to say, "I'm sorry, I'm sorry for all the years I wasn't there for you. I'm sorry for all the special moments I've missed in your life. I'm sorry for not being a dad when that is what I should have been doing all along. I'm sorry I didn't fight for you. I'm sorry...I'm sorry, baby girl."

Hearing him say sorry so many times brings another knot to her stomach and her joy is shaded with anger. Those things he's apologizing for should have made him want to be there and he wasn't which makes her feel unwanted. She cries, "So, why didn't you look for me? I needed you. I needed my daddy and you weren't there. I needed your love to guide me and protect me, but you left, as if I didn't even matter."

He presses his hand against her hair, "Baby girl, there is so much I need to share with you. So much I need to tell you, but right now I just want to cherish this moment, because I've looked forward to this day for years."

For Jazzman, everything he is saying is just pissing her off even more as she thinks, *if he wanted to see me, why didn't he look for me? Why didn't he come back a couple of years after he left? It took Tyson to look for him. TYSON...Tyson did this for me? I can't believe he did this for me. WOW!!! What an amazing man.*

Tony says, "Jazzman are you okay? Jazzman?"

Tony gently shakes Jazzman out of her daze.

"I'm sorry. I was just thinking of Tyson and what he must have gone through to track you down. That was really nice of him to do." Jazzman is still in awe of her friend.

Tony responds, "He seems like a very special man in your life."

"He is! Dad, I'm sorry, but it's not going to be easy to forgive you. I needed you and I don't understand what kind of man leaves his child. What kind of man does not look for his daughter, knowing that I would have to grow up and learn about guys on my own? Didn't you worry about guys taking advantage of your little girl?"

Tony's face turns flush and he feels out of place. "You're right—"

Jazzman raises her voice, "I'm not asking you for your approval, I need to know. Why? Why did you leave?"

"I was selfish. I'm sorry. I know that I can't take back the years that I wasn't there for you. I know it may take many years to gain your trust, but I'm here now. I'm not going anywhere if you'll allow me to be a part of your life. There is so much we need to discuss, there is so much I need to tell you, but I don't want to overwhelm you."

"Tell me, how come you didn't go to mommy's funeral. You left flowers at her grave. I was so mad when you did that and didn't even look for me to see how I was doing!"

"By the time I found out, it was too late to make it to the funeral. As soon as I found out, I booked a flight and went to the cemetery."

Somehow hearing that eased the pain around her heart that she is feeling and asks, "If you would have found out on time, would you have gone to the wake?"

"Honestly, Jazz, no, but for your sake. My mom passed away years ago and I know that feeling. I would not have wanted to add to the emotions that were already stirring in you. I would not have wanted to add to the fire and rage you were already feeling. I could not take that moment of putting your mom to rest, away from you. You spent your whole life with her and you deserved that time with her. Does that make sense?"

Jazzman feels saddened by his words. "As much as it hurts, I do understand. I get it. I miss her so much, daddy."

Tony's eyes tear up. He reaches out to comfort her and she allows him to hold her. "I know, baby girl. I know. She was a beautiful woman. I'm so sorry for all the wrong I did. I'm sorry for all the pain I caused.

I wish I could take it all back. I know you may not believe me, but I loved your mother so much and when I heard that she passed away I was torn. I cried for days. The guilt consumes me, because I wanted to tell her I was sorry for so long and I didn't get the chance to."

"You really did hurt her and you hurt me, too, by never looking for me." She looks at him to see what he has to say.

"I know I did. I was a selfish man. I'm so sorry."

Jazzman continues, "I still have a lot of anger towards you, but a piece of me is happy that you're here. I know the little bit of happiness that I feel is part of the emptiness that I feel for mommy passing. I'm sorry, I'm not trying to hurt your feelings, it's just the truth."

"You do not have to apologize for your feelings. You deserve to be angry. That's one of the reasons why I feared coming back into your life...I...I didn't want to disrupt your flow. Like I said, there is so much I need to tell you."

For several minutes they continue talking, getting past the initial hurt and slowly building trust by learning about one another. It is extremely hard for Jazzman and Tony is patient with her. Not once does he justify his actions, which helps Jazzman to appreciate his honesty, even when it hurts her. Finally, Jazzman's curiosity brings her to ask, "Do I have any brothers or sisters?"

A sad expression takes hold of Tony's face. "No, you don't...It's just you and me kid. Besides, I did not want to risk ruining another kid's life."

"I see." Jazzman is sad for still being an only child because growing up she always felt lonely. At the same time, she is happy knowing she doesn't have to share her dad. That thought brings her to ask, "Are you married?"

"No. As you may know a musician's life is hectic and long-term relationships are a hard thing to maintain in this industry."

Jazzman replies, "Do I ever. My fiancé is a musician."

"I heard. I read about it and Tyson confirmed it."

At that moment, Tyson walks back into the courtyard. "How are things over here? Jazz, are you okay?"

"I'm good."

Tyson scratches his head. "I hate to rush due to the circumstances, but we have to get going to the festival."

Tony adds, "I have to go there, too. I have to perform in a few hours." He hands her a piece of paper. "Here are all the ways to get in touch with me."

"Thank you." Jazzman takes the paper. She pulls out a business card and writes her personal contact information as she says, "Here's how you can reach me."

"I would like to see you before you go back to Miami. Maybe we can have lunch or dinner."

Jazzman is happy that he wants to see her again. "I would like that a lot."

They hold one another for several minutes. They are heart broken as they have to end their time together. They are hoping that since they are heading to the same place, they will have more time to talk. Tony tells Jazzman he will be playing the trumpet for one of the local bands. It's a band Tyson recommended for Jazzman to hear, 'Soul 2 Blues'. She loved the name when she first heard it and now that she knows her dad is part of the group, she is even more excited to hear them perform. At the same time, she grows a little hesitant because she is unsure if he is trying to smooth talk his way into a record deal or if he is really sincere about getting to know her. It's something she has to keep in the back of her mind, because she has seen people get used in the music industry.

Today's list of performers brought more people out to the fair grounds. Jazzman and Tyson are impressed with the bands that perform. That evening, deliberations are even harder as they decide which ones they will bring to the attention of Charles. They finally decide on shaving their original three down to two and adding another three from what they heard today.

The Jazz Festival began in the 1970's in New Orleans, and now the festival welcomes over several hundred thousand music lovers. It's a friendly atmosphere. From contemporary Jazz to traditional

Jazz, from crawfish to southern home-style foods, from local venues to exotic vendors, the festival has a way of bringing southern culture to life. Jazzman and Tyson are excited about the birth of Jazz music at their label and know it will improve the label's revenue. Now they can enjoy these festivities for years to come.

ༀ

NEW ORLEANS, LA
Jazzman and Tony

While Tyson is out on a hot date with a girl he met the night before, Jazzman is out having lunch with her dad. During lunch, Jazzman begins to learn about her dad's childhood. She learns about where he was born in Carolina, Puerto Rico, and the challenges he faced growing up in America. She learns that people born from that town who settle in the United States are usually mistaken as African Americans.

He brings her back to his younger years. "I moved to America as a young boy with my sister, my mom and dad. We moved because my mother's family was already settled here. She wanted to be close to them, and provide a better living for your aunt and me. When I moved to America my life and the world I knew changed. So, in a foreign place, I ended up with a low self-esteem and so did my sister."

Jazzman asks, "How old were you and why did it change you?"

Tony continues, "I was twelve when I moved here and life changed for me. First, let me say, my mom, your grandmother, was beautiful and a lighter complexion than your grandfather. However, my sister and I were dark and we could pass for African American. Your aunt and I always felt out of place at family gatherings. It bothered us because our family was supposed to have our backs, but we felt so out of place. We were never included in the family activities with our cousins."

Jazzman interrupts, "Wow, that must have been so hard for you and lonely."

He explains, "It was and it was no better at school. I thought that by hanging with my black friends at school, I would blend in and feel a sense of belonging. However, I felt the backlash with them as well because although I looked black I really wasn't and that is just the way it was. My sister and I felt so segregated in a world where segregation already existed. However, after time we felt more connected with our black friends and it was one of the best things that could have ever happened to me."

Jazzman is curious, "How so?"

He is content that she is interested in what he has to say about his childhood. "My best friend's father was a jazz musician and that began my curiosity, as well as my appreciation for the music. Obviously, you know now I live for it!" He realizes what he just said. He notices the way Jazzman grows uneasy with his statement.

However, she relaxes and says, "It's okay. Continue."

He explains, "No, that wasn't okay. I'm sorry. This is all new to me, but Jazzman if there is anything I can teach you, it would be to speak your mind. Don't allow what I did to your mother be a way of living for you. You fight back and don't let anyone hurt you. Don't bottle it all in because of me and what I did. I was wrong."

His message hits home to her current situation, with learning to say no. Jazzman grows sad and feels uneasy. "It's hard for me, but I'm learning. Please continue your story about your appreciation for jazz music. I need to hear that right now."

Tony understands and at that moment he sees so much of her mother in her. He sees her vulnerability. He respects her request. "It all started in the back alleys that were prevalent in the ghettos. Those times called for some soulful blues and the only place I could grasp the knowledge of the music was in the alleys of south side Chicago. In each alley there stood at least one back door to a bar where jazz music could be heard. One of my friends, Ronnie, worked for a drug dealer. He would take me on runs with him. Ronnie would go out of his way to make his last run of the day at this bar called, Bluez. He would do this for me. Ronnie would stay at the bar for hours and leave me at the back door to learn the music, by hearing the beats."

Jazzman asks, "Weren't you afraid of getting caught or getting in trouble?"

Tony smiles. "Nah, if anyone were to ask, 'what's a young boy like you doing out at this time of night?' My response would be 'I'm waiting on Ronnie'. That person would know to leave well enough alone and not ask any more questions. Ronnie saw me as a little brother. He saw my full potential. I felt close to Ronnie because I never got that from my male cousins and I always felt like an outcast. As a young boy I was taught to not share my emotions, so jazz music was a way to express what was bottled up inside. Since I was able to release what I was feeling I grew a connection to the music. I love the way jazz music tells a story. Music was and is my salvation."

Jazzman had sometimes wondered why she reacted the way she did to music, and why she felt such a connection to it. She now feels like she found her answer in this moment with her father. When he is telling her the story, she feels a huge weight being lifted off her shoulders and it's at this moment she feels a connection to him. It feels good and she appreciates that they have something in common, music. She jokes with him, "I see you get your music appreciation from me."

He smiles. He is happy that through the pain he can see her beautiful smile. He is also happy that she gave him a chance to change the subject, because he didn't want to tell her too much about his childhood. "You have her smile. She was beautiful, Jazzman, just like you. I'm sorry for what I did to her and I'm so sorry for what I did to you. I robbed you of a normal childhood and I robbed you of a happy childhood. I'm not sure you will ever forgive me. I'm not sure I want that forgiveness, because I don't feel I deserve it. However, what I do want is time to get to know you and be there for you from this moment on, the way I should have been there all along. Please let me be here for you. At least think about it."

She replies, "Baby steps, dad."

Hearing that meant the world to him, "Thank you for calling me, dad." He chokes up as he says it and she reaches for his hand. She shares his emotions, and also reaches for a much needed hug. He takes her in his arms and holds her as she cries and cries. Many tears are shed for their loss, their pain and the realization of this needed moment. A void they knew existed. A void filled with love that they both so desperately need.

As Tony holds his daughter he tells her, "I'm sorry for my anger and how I let it take control of me. I'm sorry I didn't get the help I needed. There is a saying, 'You hurt the ones you love the most' and that is what I did. Someone once asked me, 'Why do we treat complete strangers better than we treat loved ones?' I didn't have an answer for that person, but that person made me see what I've done for so many years. I'm so polite to complete strangers. I lose sight of that politeness when I'm having a bad day and I hurt the ones closest to me. I'm still learning to stop that bad behavior."

He continues explaining, "You know, Jazz, being in this business for so long I've had so many women throwing themselves at me, even married women. It brought me to question your mother's love."

Jazzman pulls away from him stating, "Don't you dare talk bad about mom. Don't you dare."

He grows nervous. "Oh no, Jazz, I wasn't going to. I just want to explain what was wrong with me. It had nothing to do with her and everything to do with me. I was wrong. I will never talk bad about her. She was the most amazing woman I loved. I think one of the reasons why I reacted the way I did with her was that I felt like I didn't deserve her love. In some ways, I thought the only way to keep her was through self-destruction. In the end, we all lost because I was a coward and not a real man. I wasn't there for my family. My family needed me and I...I....I'm sorry, Jazz. I'm sorry. I know I must sound like a broken record."

They both take a moment to just be silent with their feelings. It was a moment that was needed.

Then he goes on explaining, "Jazz, missing out on your life has brought such shame to my being. You know it took several years for me to realize that what I was doing was wrong. It wasn't until several years after I left you, that I met a woman who helped me see that I should at least attempt to be there for you."

When he says that, Jazzman appears confused, until Tony reaches into his bag and gives her all the returned mail he received from Jazzman's mother. There were cards and letters that stated 'Return to Sender'. It overwhelmed her and she begins to cry. It's the first time that she feels betrayed by her mother and anger towards her. She feels like an eighteen-wheeler just hit her, head on. All these years she thought that her father did not love her. She thinks back to all the times she called him a coward. He did love her. He did think of her and now he proved it to her. She feels some of the anger she has built towards him begin to chip away. She still has her reservations, but she feels more at ease in making a connection with a total stranger by getting to know her father. She will have to start from scratch with him, but his efforts from the letters he wrote gives her the reassurance she needs to take it one day at a time. She will give herself permission to open up to him. She can't wait to go home and read every piece of mail. "Thank you, this means a lot to me."

Her thoughts from yesterday on questioning his motives come flashing back to her and she now knows she can put those thoughts to rest. Although Jazzman feels some anger towards her mother, she does not harbor any ill will toward her because she knows that her mother was just trying to protect them. After all he was still abusive and Jazzman's mom could not ignore the person he became when angry. Still, she can't disregard the fact that she was robbed of her relationship with her dad and she needed him. She always remembered grandmother's comments that whatever adults go through, kids should not have to carry the burden of, and Jazzman feels like she did just that. It tears her up inside. There were times in her life when she felt so lost and it was usually connected to the men in her life. She worried about losing herself in a relationship and when things got too close for comfort, Jazzman usually was the first one to bounce. For the first time, she recognizes she is the one who usually sabotaged the relationship when things were going well. Now, she realizes the root cause may just be with her father's decision to leave her.

Jazzman feels a new sense of being beginning to bloom. Having her dad back in her life may now put things she's questioned into better perspective. After lunch, the two confirm that Tony will be able to go see her in Miami. They know this is a new beginning for them. They decide to take it one day at a time, knowing it will be essential for building their bond.

⌒◯

NEW ORLEANS, LA
Jazzman and Tyson

Tyson and Jazzman made plans to meet after their lunch dates one last time before heading to the airport. Tyson is in his room waiting for her call. When the telephone rings, he picks up informing her right away, "It's been a hard day and my date was wack. I need some love. Heck, I'll even provide the drinks, so you can blame it on the alcohol."

He can hear Jazzman giggling. She has been feeling a strange emotion toward him ever since she saw women throwing themselves at him. She reacts to that feeling by responding, "Well then, I'll provide the pleasure. One stop solution right here!"

Tyson likes her response. "Really? Drive-thru or full service?"

Jazzman smiles, "Full service, baby, with extra benefits."

Tyson inquiries even further, "Nice! Nine to five or twenty-four hours?"

"Twenty-four hours, seven days a week, including holidays."

Tyson's 'Colgate' smile is in full bloom. "In any climate?"

Jazzman blushes as she responds, "Especially when the roads are slippery and wet."

He is still smiling and another part of his body is rising to the occasion in agreement with her response, "I'm getting hot."

"I beg to differ. I believe you need me first to make you hot and don't worry I have A/C to cool you off." She can't believe what she just said. She wants to take it back, but it's too late.

"Show me what you got."

"I'll see you in a few minutes. I have one request." She is extremely nervous.

"Name it and your wish is my command." Tyson can sense she has a lot on her mind to be reacting to him in this manner.

She whispers, "Honestly, what I need right now is for you to play it again."

He whispers back, "I got you."

When she arrives at his suite, he did just that. He plays, "At Last." As the melody begins and before she can ask, 'Would you do me the honor of dancing with me'? He already has her in his arms. She is so lost and he helps her find her way. He knows he is needed and he knows that in his arms his friend feels safe and secure. He senses her pain and he attempts to mend it by just simply being there for her. He is giving her the attention she so desperately needs to feel appreciated as a woman. No drama, just the essence of two souls connecting.

NEW ORLEANS AIRPORT
Jazzman and Tyson

Jazzman wonders what life would have been like if she and Tyson were together. He knows her well and he questions her motives when no one else will. For any major decision in her life, he knows how to bring to the surface her true senses. He does this by asking her hard questions that make her think and in her answer he understands her state of mind. He has truly outdone himself with bringing her father back into her life. He helped with all the anxiety she would have endured going through the process of finding him. He helped remove all those emotions, so that she can start with a clean slate when seeing her dad for the first time.

As they get on the plane, Jazzman locks her gaze with Tyson and says, "I love you, Tyse!" They both know what she means, but due to the circumstances no other words are shared.

As they fasten their seat belts, and as the saying goes... 'What happens in New Orleans, stays in New Orleans'. What happened at the hotel before they checked out?

The pilot calls out, "Flight attendants prepare for takeoff."

~~ *Is This The End?* ~~

About The Author

I rene Melo was born and raised in Hartford, Connecticut. Active in the entertainment industry since the age of fifteen, she began by volunteering at Hartford Public Access Television Station, where she assisted with the production of a local show called *Reggae Vibes*.

While attending Emerson College, where she would go on to earn a bachelor's degree in film production, Melo interned for productions such as *Yo! MTV Raps* in New York and New Line Cinema in California. For her senior year, she wrote, produced, and directed a documentary entitled *School Smarts: A Positive Outlook to the Negative Views* that interviewed students, faculty, and parents within the Hartford school system.

Melo published her first novel, *How Far Would You Go?*, in 2007.

Currently in the corporate world of business, Melo enjoys writing and volunteering for Habitat for Humanity in her spare time.

For more information, visit www.irenemelo.com or email Irene at Irene.Melo@yahoo.com.